An Investigation
of
ANGELS

by
Wynelle F. Main

Scriptures taken from the
HOLY BIBLE, NEW INTERNATIONAL VERSION
Copyright 1973, 1978, 1984
International Bible Society

IBSN: 0-89137-462-0

The author wishes to express grateful appreciation to the following people for their assistance and encouragement:

Jean Keplinger
Mary Ann Cox
Charles Freeman
Michael A. Sparks
Elizabeth Lassetter
Kay Eddins
Sandra Mackey
Robert C. Main

Table of Contents

Introduction 1

Chapter One   Occupation: Angel 6

Chapter Two   Job Description 22

Chapter Three   Reported Sightings 42

Chapter Four   Organization Chart 54

Chapter Five   Christ and the Angels 71

Chapter Six   Influence of the Jews 87

Chapter Seven   Angels in Art and Literature 101

Chapter Eight   False Accusations 116

Chapter Nine   Angels and Other Religions 130

Chapter Ten   The Angel of the Lord 143

Chapter Eleven   The Death Angel? 159

Chapter Twelve   My Guardian Angel? 175

Chapter Thirteen   Evil Angels 190

Conclusion 213

Bibliography 217

Introduction

Confusion About Angels

What would you do if you overheard someone making a statement that totally contradicted what you have been taught on a particular Bible subject? You might begin to question others to find reinforcement for your beliefs, or you might start to study to prove to yourself that you were correct. That is how this investigation began. I became aware of the confusion in the world, the religious world in particular, regarding the angels. The origin, characteristics, description, duties, and classification of angels are often misrepresented to us. One extreme is to attribute everything for which there is no obvious explanation to the operation of angels. The other is to discard completely the belief in angels as myth.

ARE WE AVOIDING THE SUBJECT?

Many books are available on the subjects of satanic worship, witchcraft, demons, exorcism, and the occult. Very few books are being published on the theme of angels. Even though there is a prevailing fascination with the topic, few sermons are preached and few Bible lessons are taught on the subject of angels.

The teachings of the Bible, especially the Old Testament, present angels as an indefinite, somewhat vague group of beings. There is no detailed description of these non-human messengers; even their origin is mentioned only indirectly. Although there is a desire to learn more about the angels, we must not go beyond what is revealed by Scripture. To try to answer questions concerning heaven's angels which are not answered in the Bible is a total waste of time.

SOURCES OF FALSE INFORMATION

Outside the teaching of Scripture there has always been a human tendency to enhance information about the angels. We have given them human characteristics, abilities, and limitations. They are systematized and organized into precise ranks and classifications, and the events of their scriptural past are so enhanced that they have become almost unrecognizable.

What is the origin of the incorrect information which is being spread so effectively throughout the world today? It may have begun with the captivity of the Jews and their exposure to Babylonian and Persian civilization and religion. This was further promoted by the addition of Jewish legend and custom which increased the role and significance of angels beyond biblical teaching. The mortal tendency to attribute human form and qualities to spirit beings was also a contributing factor.

The Eastern religions, such as Zoroastrianism and Islam, teach the existence of intermediaries that go between the mortal and divine realms. The angels found in the writings of these religions do not correspond with the teachings of Scripture, but confusing similiarities are found. Some of the untruths that we have blindly accepted, generation after generation, may date back to ancient times.

Some of the religious groups in western culture today are also very creative in their doctrines concerning angels. Specific reference is made to the Church of Jesus Christ of Latter-day Saints and Jehovah's Witnesses. The instruction of these groups regarding angels is unlike the customary Christian beliefs. The first mentioned group supplements the Bible with additional sacred books which add to the teaching on angels. Scriptures pertaining to the angels receive an unusual interpretation by the other sect.

In the myths of ancient Greece and Rome we find descriptions of winged gods and goddesses. These descriptions of mythological characters were used by the artists of the Middle Ages and the Renaissance when painting angels. Apparently this occurred because biblical information was found to be somewhat obscure. We can see the results in the portrayal of angels in both paintings and sculpture. The angels and the winged figures of mythology are so similar that they appear to be the same characters. This has caused difficulty in the understanding of biblical angels.

The literature of the thirteenth to the eighteenth centuries introduced a complicated and detailed order of the angels of heaven and the angels of hell. Although this is very loosely based on the Bible, it is in no way authoritative. Yet, its confusing information on angels has added to our perplexity.

When information pertaining to angels is taken from a wide range and variety of human sources the resulting knowledge is unacceptable. Over the centuries, cultural influences, history, mythology, art, literature, philosophy, and even pagan religions, have contributed to our thinking and clouded our minds on this essential theme.

SOURCE OF TRUE INFORMATION

The source of true information on angels is limited to the Bible. We recognize the Holy Scriptures as the only authoritative source of information concerning heaven's angels. The study of angels is not a matter of scientific or philosophical learning, but the examination of inspired writing revealed in God's Word.

If we want information about current events we read the newspaper or watch television reports. When the spelling or definition of a word is in question, we consult a dictionary. When we are learning to repair a household item or prepare a new food, we may consult a how-to book or a recipe. If we want to know about God's angels, we should go to God's Book.

The angels were created and employed to act as go-betweens from God to man. They are an innumerable group of spirit beings whose occupation is "angel." Various biblical references present angels as dreadful, forceful and terrifying. In these passages, angels are described as: "awesome," "frightening," "mighty," or "powerful." Yet, the contemporary picture of an angel is a delicate, beautiful creature.

When did the image change? How did we go from a ministering spirit and messenger of God, to the "treetop angel" of today? It could not be more successful if a propaganda campaign were carried on to misinform us. Apparently this subtle transformation has been in progress for hundreds, perhaps thousands of years.

WOULD A WORLDLY GROUP ACCEPT MISREPRESENTATION?

Suppose an organized group in the world were being misrepresented in a similar way. Would some "macho" group like, perhaps the steelworkers, or the longshoremen of this nation accept being labeled as: beautiful, delicate, effeminate, soft-spoken, and gentle? What if the entire meaning and importance of their profession were being wrongly defined? Can you imagine the extent to which their union leaders would go to correct the distorted image? They might even seek the services of a public relations company. This book is an endeavor to improve the "Public Relations" of the angels and reveal a more accurate picture of these spirit messengers of God to our minds.

GOAL OF THIS STUDY

We are disadvantaged by our lack of understanding of the angel-ambassadors of God. Therefore, the goal is to correct our imperfect view of the nature and ministry of angels, to better understand the truth, and to be able to recognize error when we see it. In order to accomplish this, we will begin with a complete, Scriptural study of the subject of angels. Unless indicated, the references are quoted from the **NEW INTERNATIONAL VERSION of the HOLY BIBLE.** We will examine the teaching of the Bible

4

on angels and investigate their misrepresentation in other fields of study.

The study of angels, or angelology, has been a universal theme throughout the ages. Its great significance in Christian teaching is substantiated by 265 verses of reference in the Old Testament and 227 verses in the New Testament. This includes reference to angels who are called by names such as holy ones, heavenly beings, men, hosts of heaven, multitudes of heaven, mighty ones, heavenly hosts, messengers, thrones, powers, rulers, and authorities. Also included are references to particular angels, Michael and Gabriel, as well as other heavenly beings, cherubim, seraphs, and living creatures. This study will show, however, that far more detailed information about angels is found in secular sources than in the Bible.

EFFECT OF EXPOSURE TO MISINFORMATION

Since each of us is a product of the cultural influences that surround us, we cannot avoid some effect from the wealth of information to which we are exposed. When we read the Bible, as with any other printed matter, we form visual images based on what we comprehend. Therefore, it is difficult to separate nonbiblical knowledge from scriptural facts. The images of angels are formed from all related knowledge which is stored in memory. In this way, bits of related but foreign information, from folklore to fine art, distort the true likeness.

Through an examination of the Scripture, we will find a realistic representation of God's messengers, and contrast this with the manner in which angels are represented in the uninspired products of man's creativity. By understanding the origin of the material, we will be able to evaluate its effect on our mental image and our understanding of the angels.

Chapter One

Occupation: Angel

The word "angel," as it was used in the Bible, is not so much the name of a being as a description of the service this spirit being performed. Angel is not what he *was* but what he *did*. He was an employee of God, in the occupation of angel.

GOD'S MESSENGER SERVICE

God communicated with man through the agency or representation of angel messengers. The English word "angel" is derived from the Greek word for messenger. That word is *angelos* and it means "a messenger." The Hebrew word is *mal'akh*, which means "to send, to minister, or to employ." In Old Testament times, the word did not have the exclusive meaning of a spirit being or messenger of God. The original languages used this same word whether referring to mortal messengers or heavenly ones. The word was also used to indicate prophets and priests. Only the circumstances or the context determined how the word was translated. Examples:

human messenger - After John's messengers left, Jesus began to speak to the crowd about John: . . . [Luke 7:24].

prophet - The Lord, the God of their fathers, sent word to them through his messengers again and again, because he had pity on his people and on his dwelling place [2 Chronicles 36:15].

priest - For the lips of a priest ought to preserve knowledge, and from his mouth men should seek instruction—because he is the messenger of the Lord Almighty [Malachi 2:7].

heavenly messenger - In the visions I saw while lying in my bed, I looked, and there before me was a messenger, a holy one, coming down from heaven [Daniel 4:13].

For better understanding, the Jews began to use the word *malakh* to refer to only heavenly messengers after the time the Old Testament was written.

Angels are not always identified by the name "angel." In Scripture they are also called: "hosts of heaven," "mighty ones," "holy ones," "heavenly beings," and "sons of God."

OUR DEFINITION

The word *angel* literally means messenger, but we have given it many meanings. In our vocabulary today, the entire definition of the word has changed. When one is called an angel nowadays, no one thinks he or she is being called a messenger.

Consider the current use of these words and phrases:

little angel . . . . infant
real angel . . . . good person
angel . . . . theater's financial backer
angel of mercy . . . . nurse
angel dust . . . . hallucinogenic drug
angel food . . . . light textured cake
angel hair . . . . holiday decoration
angel breath . . . . type of cloud
angel biscuit . . . . yeast roll

The word "angel," as it is currently used, instead of referring to a messenger of God, is more often a term of endearment, or one stressing unusual delicacy, purity, innocence, or kindness. A person with desirable qualities such as modesty, goodness, honesty, or unselfishness is thought of as "angelic."

Some people place angels in the same category as elves, gremlins, and leprechauns, while others equate angels with Santa and the Tooth Fairy. Neither of these is an appropriate way to classify the angels of God.

7

In your mind, contrast biblical angels with angels as we imagine them today. The Bible often describes angels as dreadful, forceful and terrifying; yet, the contemporary picture of an angel is a delicate, beautiful creature. The typical visual image of an angel is a sentimental, beautiful, feminine creature with long, blond hair, wings, and a halo. It is often thought that this being is someone who once lived a righteous life on earth. We imagine the angel spends much time playing a harp, resting on clouds, and flying to choir practice.

NOT ALL ANGELS ARE GOOD

Although we most often associate the word "angel" with goodness, the name was also applied to evil messengers. We find two groups of evil angels in Scripture. One of these was the angels who sinned and were sent to hell. The other group of evil angels found in the Bible is the angels of Satan. Both of these categories will be discussed in Chapter 13, "Evil Angels."

ORIGIN OF ANGELS

What is the origin of angels? Although the Bible is not explicit in answering this question, we do know that angels did not always exist. Angels were created by God, through His Son, at a time before the creation of the world. Although the angels are not specifically mentioned in the detailed account of creation given in Genesis, we find other reference to their creation.

> Praise him, all his angels, praise him, all his heavenly hosts. . . .Let them praise the name of the Lord, for he commanded and they were created [Psalm 148:2,5].

In this call to praise God, the angels and heavenly hosts are listed with sun, moon, stars, heavens, and waters above the skies as being created at His command.

Jesus was God's representative in the creation of the entire universe. This includes the things we can see on earth, and the unseen, or invisible things of heaven, such as the angels.

In the beginning was the Word, and the Word was with God, and the Word was God. He was with God in the beginning. Through him all things were made; without him nothing was made that has been made [John 1:1-3].

The Word became flesh and made his dwelling among us. We have seen his glory, the glory of the One and Only, who came from the Father, full of grace and truth [John 1:14].

He is the image of the invisible God, the firstborn over all creation. For by him all things were created: things in heaven and on earth, visible and invisible, whether thrones or powers or rulers or authorities; all things were created by him and for him. He is before all things, and in him all things hold together [Colossians 1:15-17].

"In the beginning, God created the heavens and the earth" [Genesis 1:1]. According to some scholars, the word "heavens" in this verse included the entire body of spiritual creatures. Reference to the "beginning" indicated that nothing had been created before this time. This interpretation would establish the time of the creation of angels, at the very outset of creation.

Thus the heavens and the earth were completed in all their vast array. By the seventh day God had finished the work he had been doing; so on the seventh day he rested from all his work [Genesis 2:1-2].

Since the home of the angels is heaven, it is believed that the completion of the heavens included the creation of angels.

We find additional information to fix the time of the creation of angels when we read from the Book of Job.

Where were you when I laid the earth's foundation? Tell me, if you understand. Who marked off its dimensions? Surely you know! Who stretched a measuring line across it? On what were its footings set, or who laid its cornerstone — while the morning stars sang together and all the angels shouted for joy? [Job 38:4-7].

As God talked to Job about the creation of the world, He indicated that the angels were present when He "laid the earth's foundation." Therefore, they were created before God began to create the earth.

Paul started his prayer for the Ephesians by mentioning God's family. Just as we are a part of God's family on earth, the angels are a part of His family in heaven.

> For this reason I kneel before the Father, from whom His whole family in heaven and on earth derives its name [Ephesians 3:14-15].

NUMBER OF ANGELS

How many angels did God create? There has been a great deal of speculation about this question. It is not a mathematical problem that can be solved with a formula or a calculation. Neither is it a theological question that can be answered by the study of Scripture. It is a philosophical question and involves speculation. We cannot arrive at a reliable answer so why guess?

> He said: "The Lord came from Sinai and dawned over them from Seir; he shone forth from Mount Paran. He came with myriads of holy ones from the south, from his mountain slopes" [Deuteronomy 33:2].

The term "holy ones," refers to God's holy angels. This same term is used elsewhere to mean the Israelites or the saints. The word "myriad" means that a thing has innumerable parts. So "myriads of holy ones," refers to countless numbers of angels.

In Gethsemane, Jesus was betrayed by a kiss from Judas. One of His companions drew a sword to defend Jesus, and cut off the right ear of Malchus, the high priest's servant. John wrote that this zealous protector of Jesus was Simon Peter (John 18:10). Jesus spoke of the large number as well as the availability of angels, when He said to him:

> Do you think I cannot call on my Father, and He will at once put at my disposal more than twelve legions of angels? [Matthew 26:53].

A legion in the Roman army was six thousand soldiers. Jesus said that it was possible for God to immediately dispatch seventy-two thousand angels to defend His Son.

In describing the heavenly city of Jerusalem, the dwelling place of God and His angels, the writer of Hebrews said,

> But you have come to Mount Zion, to the heavenly Jerusalem, the city of the living God. You have come to thousands upon thousands of angels in joyful assembly [Hebrews 12:22].

The King James Version gives meaning by translating these words, "an innumerable company of angels." In this description of heaven, the term "thousands upon thousands" expressed an infinitely large number of angels who are assembled around the throne of God, joyfully praising Him.

John also described the population of heaven. He saw a number of angels which was too great to be counted and they were assembled around the throne of God.

> Then I looked and heard the voice of many angels, numbering thousands upon thousands, and ten thousand times ten thousand. They encircled the throne and the living creatures and the elders [Revelation 5:11].

God's angels cannot be counted, tallied, or numbered. We are given no information concerning the total number of angels. We do not find any evidence that God continued to renew His supply of angels. The number He created in the beginning was, apparently, an eternal supply, and would not ever require supplements or additions. There is no loss in the number of angels through death, because angels do not die. Angels are not a race which regenerates and multiplies by giving birth to offspring as humans do. There is no record of God extending the number of angels He originally created. There is certainly nothing to say that a righteous person becomes an angel after death, or that babies are angels before they are born. Human beings never were angels and they do not become angels when they die. Our goal in heaven is not to become angels.

CHARACTERISTICS OF ANGELS

The characteristics of angels are not specifically listed in a particular passage of Scripture. Finding the attributes and distinctions which are specific to the angels is something like fitting together the pieces of a jigsaw puzzle. The following characteristics are the qualities and traits which are found to apply to the angels. They are features which are representative of angels and are substantiated by Scripture.

MASCULINE OR FEMININE?

The terms "masculine" and "feminine" do not apply to angels as they do not have sexuality. In Scripture, angels are always referred to in the masculine gender. Masculine pronouns are always used to refer to the angels. Although neuter forms were available in the original languages, the masculine form was used in reference to angels. Apparently the neuter and female forms were inappropriate to describe these beings. The only two angels who were named in Scripture, Michael and Gabriel, have masculine names. Angels, however, are not men nor were they ever men.

Even though angels appeared in human form when bringing God's messages to men, they do not have physical bodies as men do. Perhaps these appearances on earth in human form are the reason we often think of angels as having physical bodies. To make this assumption is to restrict the angels and burden them with human deficiencies, inadequacies, and limitations.

When an angel appeared to deliver a message from God, the emphasis was on the message, not the messenger. In order for invisible spirit beings to be seen by mortal eyes, and grasped by human intelligence, it was necessary for them to make use of a form that the limited mind of mortals could comprehend. When angels appeared in human form, they took on physical bodies. They are, however, spirits, not men. In spite of the contemporary perception of femininity, Scripture teaches nothing of female angels.

IMMORTAL ANGELS

God has always existed—He is eternal. At some time which is not specified, the angels were created. They cannot be called eternal as God is eternal, because they did not always exist. The angels are immortal since they are not subject to physical death. At death, we are separated from our physical bodies, and at the resurrection, we will receive a spiritual body. Angels are spirits and they do not possess physical bodies. Their existence is immortal in the sense that they do not suffer death as we do.

> But those who are considered worthy of taking part in that age and in the resurrection from the dead will neither marry nor be given in marriage, and they can no longer die; for they are like the angels. . . [Luke 20:35-36].

The word used here for "like angels" is *isangelos*, a compound of a Greek term (*isos*) meaning like, equal, or corresponding to, and the word "angel." This word represents the circumstances of people who are resurrected from the dead, and are not subject to normal situations of life on earth, such as marriage. Some have misunderstood this to mean that we will become angels in the resurrection.

Similar passages are found in Matthew and Mark, where they are preceded by a statement to the Sadducees that they made a mistake because they did not know the Scriptures, "or the power of God."

> At the resurrection people will neither marry nor be given in marriage; they will be like the angels in heaven [Matthew 22:30].

> When the dead rise, they will neither marry nor be given in marriage; they will be like the angels in heaven [Mark 12:25].

This is in answer to a question put to Jesus by the Sadducees, in argument against the resurrection. They contrived an imaginary case about a certain woman who

13

had seven husbands in succession. Whose wife would she be at the resurrection? The reference to angels here is to teach that at the time of resurrection, we will be like the angels in that we will not marry, as they do not; and that we will be immortal, as they are. It does not teach that we will become angels.

INTELLIGENT ANGELS

We do not find that the Scripture gauges the intelligence of angels. The Bible does indicate that the traditional belief at the time of David assumed angels to be able to determine right and wrong. The woman whom Joab engaged to flatter David used the comparative phrase "like an angel." These verses illustrate the belief in superhuman intelligence of angels.

> And now your servant says, "May the word of my lord the king bring me rest, for my lord the king is like an angel of God in discerning good and evil. May the Lord your God be with you" [2 Samuel 14:17].

> Your servant Joab did this to change the present situation. My lord has wisdom like that of an angel of God—he knows everything that happens in the land [2 Samuel 14:20].

Mephibosheth, the son of Jonathan, spoke to David in a complimentary way in this verse.

> ... My lord the king is like an angel of God; so do whatever pleases you [2 Samuel 19:27].

Even though the intelligence of angels is greater than the intelligence of human beings, their knowledge is limited. One thing they do not know was stated by Jesus when He spoke of His return.

> No one knows about that day or hour, not even the angels in heaven, nor the Son, but only the Father [Matthew 24:36].

STRONG ANGELS

Strong, powerful, and mighty are adjectives used in Scripture to describe angels. They are not the words we would choose to describe angels as we often imagine them today. Angels are, however, according to the Bible, able to command superhuman strength.

> Praise the Lord, you his angels, you mighty ones who do his bidding, who obey his word [Psalm 103:20].

Look at this example of the strength of an angel. Three women were going to the tomb to anoint Jesus' body. As they walked along, their main concern was the removal of the heavy stone.

> ... and they asked each other, "Who will roll the stone away from the entrance of the tomb?" [Mark 16:3].

Once the stone was put into place, in a groove at the opening of the tomb, it was very difficult to move it. The strength required for this task was provided by an angel.

> There was a violent earthquake, for an angel of the Lord came down from heaven and, going to the tomb, rolled back the stone and sat on it [Matthew 28:2].

When Paul spoke of the return of Christ he told us that "powerful angels" will accompany Him.

> ... This will happen when the Lord Jesus is revealed from heaven in blazing fire with his powerful angels [2 Thessalonians 1:7b].

Peter said that angels are "stronger and more powerful" than the false prophets who were prevalent at this time.

> ... yet even angels, although they are stronger and more powerful, do not bring slanderous accusations against such beings in the presence of the Lord [2 Peter 2:11].

John's Revelation referred to many angels. This particular one was "a mighty angel."

> And I saw a mighty angel proclaiming in a loud voice, "Who is worthy to break the seals and open the scroll?" [Revelation 5:2].

Consider the strength of this symbolic angel who was seen by John. A memorable visual image is produced by this description.

Then I saw another mighty angel coming down from heaven. He was robed in a cloud, with a rainbow above his head; his face was like the sun, and his legs were like fiery pillars. He was holding a little scroll, which lay open in his hand. He planted his right foot on the sea and his left foot on the land [Revelation 10:1-2].

In the next verse, strength which is far superior to human ability was demonstrated by this visionary angel as he carried out a symbolic act in a very spectacular way.

Then a mighty angel picked up a boulder the size of a large millstone and threw it into the sea, and said:

"With such violence the great city of Babylon will be thrown down, never to be found again" [Revelation 18:21].

INTEREST OF ANGELS

We learn from several biblical passages that angels take an interest in what is happening to man on earth. Paul felt that the apostles were on exhibition to the world, and even to angels. He implied a comparison between the apostles' experiences and the contests of gladiators in the Roman arena.

For it seems to me that God has put us apostles on display at the end of the procession, like men condemned to die in the arena. We have been made a spectacle to the whole universe, to angels as well as to men [1 Corinthians 4:9].

Angels watched as God's intentions for man unfolded. Human history presented them with a continuing picture of God's plan for man's salvation.

The curiosity and yearning of angels is seen in their desire to look into the preaching of the gospel. Even the prophets did not always understand the meaning of the things they foretold concerning Christ. Thus, they "searched intently and with the greatest care" [1 Peter 1:10].

Peter showed the sincere interest and questioning nature of angels with regard to man and his redemption.

It was revealed to them that they were not serving themselves but you, when they spoke of the things that have now been told you by those who have preached the gospel to you by the Holy Spirit sent from heaven. Even angels long to look into these things [1 Peter 1:12].

The word "long" comes from the Greek word *epithumeo*, meaning "to set the heart on, to want passionately." When the angels consider the salvation of man, strong sentiment is generated. The Greek word *parakupto*, here translated "to look into," literally means "to stoop and look intently" (W. E. Vine, *Expository Dictionary of New Testament Words*, III:11,13). The use of this word indicates the angels' extreme curiosity concerning man's salvation. They do not receive redemption through the death of Christ as we do.

For surely it is not angels He helps, but Abraham's descendants [Hebrews 2:16].

EVANGELISTIC ANGELS?

Although the angels brought God's messages to His people, He did not allow them to bring the gospel message. Although they were allowed to assist, there is no example of an angel being directly responsible for a conversion. An angel sent Philip to the Ethiopian. The angel directed Philip to go to a certain place where he met the eunuch, taught him, and baptized him.

Now an angel of the Lord said to Philip, "Go south to the road—the desert road—that goes down from Jerusalem to Gaza" [Acts 8:26].

Cornelius and his family were "devout and God-fearing" people. He gave to the poor and prayed regularly to God. He was a good man but he needed to hear the way of salvation. God sent an angel. The angel did not tell Cornelius how to be saved. Instead the angel instructed him to send for Peter, and Peter spoke to Cornelius of the Gospel.

One day at about three in the afternoon he had a vision. He distinctly saw an angel of God, who came to him and said, "Cornelius!" . . ."Now send men to

17

Joppa to bring back a man named Simon who is called Peter" [Acts 10:3,5].

God chose to send men such as Philip and Peter to preach the gospel rather than using angels for this purpose. He preferred that human messengers would teach each other. He compared them to "jars of clay" or "earthen vessels" (KJV). It was common in that time to hide one's treasures in clay jars to conceal and protect them. In this case, the "treasure" was the gospel.

But we have this treasure in jars of clay to show that this all-surpassing power is from God and not from us [2 Corinthians 4:7].

DISCIPLINED ANGELS

Peter described the boldness and arrogance of the false teachers of his time. They felt contempt for authority, whether earthly or heavenly. The angels were above such petty backbiting and they exhibited self-control and restraint.

. . .Bold and arrogant, these men are not afraid to slander celestial beings; yet even angels, although they are stronger and more powerful, do not bring slanderous accusations against such beings in the presence of the Lord [2 Peter 2:10b-11].

If ever there was a time for an angel to show a blaze of temper, it would be when contending with the devil. Jude's letter, however, tells us that the archangel Michael did not make derogatory comments even when arguing against the devil.

But even the archangel Michael, when he was disputing with the devil about the body of Moses, did not dare to bring a slanderous accusation against him, but said, "The Lord rebuke you!" [Jude verse 9].

HAPPY ANGELS

We think of angels as going about their duties in heaven in a spirit of cheerfulness. When the angels celebrated the beginning of God's creation, they demonstrated the capacity to express happiness and joy,

. . .while the morning stars sang together and all the angels shouted for joy? [Job 38:7].

Another reference used to show an occasion for the happiness of the angels is from the parable of the lost coin, recorded only in the Gospel of Luke.

In the same way, I tell you, there is rejoicing in the presence of the angels of God over one sinner who repents [Luke 15:10].

We always thought this verse said the angels rejoice. It does not. Instead, it says that the rejoicing is in their presence. The rejoicing is taking place in the presence of the angels.

It will be helpful to look at another passage which uses the same phrase in the original language.

I tell you, whoever acknowledges me before men, the Son of Man will also acknowledge him before the angels of God. But he who disowns me before men will be disowned before the angels of God [Luke 12:8-9).

In the original Greek, the words which are translated "presence of the angels" in Luke 15:10, are interpreted "before the angels" in Luke 12:9. If we assume the angels are doing the rejoicing in 15:10, shall we also assume the angels are disowning in 12:9? No! He will be disowned by God, "before the angels."

The parable of the lost sheep, which precedes the parable of the lost coin, also tells of rejoicing.

I tell you that in the same way there will be more rejoicing in heaven over one sinner who repents than over ninety-nine righteous persons who do not need to repent [Luke 15:7].

Here the same scene is described, and we attribute this rejoicing to angels, though they are not even mentioned.

The rejoicing in these verses is far more significant than the rejoicing of angels. Although it may include the angels, it is a reference to the rejoicing of God as the sinner repents and the angels are in His presence.

SUMMARY

The word "angel" simply means messenger, and was originally used for either human or heavenly messengers. We have changed the use of the word to include many other meanings. There are evil angels as well as good ones.

The angels were created by God through His Son. This occurred sometime before the creation of the world. Although we are told there are a great many angels, we cannot establish the number of angels God created. They are "an innumerable company."

The angels are neither male or female, although male pronouns and male proper names were used to refer to them. They are not mortal as we are, but will never die. They do not marry. Their intelligence may be greater than human understanding, but their knowledge is not unlimited. The angels possess enormous strength and great power. Angels are aware of what is happening to man on earth and they are inquisitive about the preaching of the gospel. Angels are not allowed to bring the gospel message to man. They are well-disciplined beings, capable of expressing their joy and gladness, but it is not recorded that they rejoice at the time a sinner repents.

REVIEW

1. What is the meaning of the word "angel"? _____

_____

2. How is the word angel used today?_____

_____

3. What is the origin of angels?_____

_____

4. When were angels created?_____

_____

5. How many angels were created? _____

_____

6. Are the angels masculine or feminine? _____

_____

7. What is the lifetime of an angel?_____

_____

8. In regard to strength, how do angels compare with humans? _____

_____

9. Do angels preach the gospel?_____
   Do they assist? _____

10. Name some characteristics of angels. _____

_____

11. Who rejoices when a sinner repents? _____

_____

NOTES

_____
_____
_____
_____
_____
_____
_____
_____
_____
_____
_____
_____
_____
_____
_____
_____
_____
_____
_____
_____
_____
_____
_____
_____

Chapter Two

Job Description

I n this chapter we shall examine the Scriptures to learn how the angels functioned in the Bible. What was the work of an angel? The Bible does not list a detailed job description but we may learn from the references to angels in Scripture, what tasks they performed in times past, what duties they are performing at present, and what they will do in the age to come.

PAST PERFORMANCE OF ANGELS

MESSENGER ANGELS

You will remember that the word "angel" describes what he does, not what he is, and that word means "messenger". Therefore, the definition is our first clue to the duties of an angel. The meaning of the word in both Hebrew and Greek is messenger, and the angels of both the Old and New Testaments acted as messengers from God to mankind.

The first time the word "angel" appeared in the Bible was when the angel of the Lord brought a message to Hagar. He told her to go back to Sarai and submit to her. He also announced that she would have a son and through him numerous descendants.

> The angel of the Lord also said to her: "You are now with child and you will have a son. You shall name him Ishmael, for the Lord has heard of your misery.

He will be a wild donkey of a man; his hand will be against everyone and everyone's hand against him, and he will live in hostility toward all his brothers" [Genesis 16:11-12].

We are going to see that many of the messages that angels brought related to the birth of a child. Manoah's wife received this message from the angel of the Lord. The message of the angel foretold the birth of her son, Samson, who became a judge of Israel.

". . .You are sterile and childless, but you are going to conceive and have a son" [Judges 13:3].

Another message associated with a child's birth was brought by an angel, to Zechariah as he was on duty as a priest serving God. He was chosen by lot as the priest to go inside the Temple that particular day to burn the incense. Outside the worshipers were praying. Zechariah was alone in the Temple when the angel Gabriel appeared beside the altar of incense. Gabriel came to bring Zechariah a message about the birth of his son John.

". . .Do not be afraid, Zechariah; your prayer has been heard. Your wife Elizabeth will bear you a son, and you are to give him the name John" [Luke 1:13].

The most famous message of all time was also delivered by the angel Gabriel. God sent him to Mary to inform her that she would conceive by the Holy Spirit and give birth to a Son. Notice that again the angel Gabriel tells the parent what to name the child.

The angel went to her and said, "Greetings, you who are highly favored! The Lord is with you. . . .You will be with child and give birth to a son, and you are to give him the name Jesus. He will be great and will be called the Son of the Most High. The Lord God will give him the throne of his father David, and he will reign over the house of Jacob forever; his kingdom will never end" [Luke 1:28; 31-33].

God chose the lowly shepherds to receive another famous message. Luke told us they were living nearby, watching their flocks, when the angel appeared to them one night in the fields.

> But the angel said to them, "Do not be afraid. I bring you good news of great joy that will be for all the people. Today in the town of David a Savior has been born to you; he is Christ the Lord. This will be a sign to you: You will find a baby wrapped in cloths and lying in a manger" [Luke 2:10-12].

The messenger angels which we have considered were apparently recognized to be God's messengers, but He used angels in various manners. God also used the angels in other ways to reveal His will to mankind. At times He had them materialize in the form of men, or appear in dreams or visions. The emphasis was on the message and not on the messenger. The messengers who came to Lot seemed to be men, however, they are identified as angels in Genesis 19:1.

> The two men said to Lot, "Do you have anyone else here — sons-in-law, sons or daughters, or anyone else in the city who belongs to you? Get them out of here because we are going to destroy this place. The outcry to the Lord against its people is so great that he has sent us to destroy it" [Genesis 19:12-13].

We usually think of a vision appearing to a person who is awake, while a dream occurs in a person's sleep. But this apparition and the dream in Daniel 2 are called by both of these names. It seems as if Nebuchadnezzar had a dream, and in the dream he saw images and visions.

An example of an angel who brought a message by appearing in a vision is described by Nebuchadnezzar to Daniel.

> In the visions I saw while lying in my bed, I looked and there before me was a messenger, a holy one, coming down from heaven [Daniel 4:13].

The Wise Men, or the "Magi," as the New International Version says, did not come to visit Jesus on the night of His birth as the shepherds did. It was much later and the family was in a house. After they were gone, this urgent message was brought to Joseph by an angel who appeared to him in a dream.

> When they had gone, an angel of the Lord appeared to Joseph in a dream. "Get up," he said, "take the child and his mother and escape to Egypt. Stay there until I tell you, for Herod is going to search for the child to kill him" [Matthew 2:13].

God's usual means of communication with Joseph was an angel who appeared in a dream. This was also the way He reassured Joseph in regard to Mary's pregnancy so that he did not divorce her. Later, when it was safe for them to return, an angel again, in a dream, informed Joseph.

God communicated with Moses in a unique way. Moses was a shepherd when he was called to become a leader of God's people. An angel appeared in the flames of a bush which burned without being consumed.

> There the angel of the Lord appeared to him in flames of fire from within a bush. Moses saw that though the bush was on fire, it did not burn up [Exodus 3:2].

INTERVENING ANGELS

God used angels as His instruments to alter circumstances, execute decisions, and punish people. One such time was when David counted his military troops. He put his confidence in manpower instead of trusting God for security. God offered him a choice of punishment and David choose three days of plague. Then God sent an angel to carry out His sentence and seventy thousand people died.

> When the angel stretched out his hand to destroy Jerusalem, the Lord was grieved because of the calamity and said to the angel who was afflicting the people, "Enough! Withdraw your hand." The angel of the Lord was then at the threshing floor of Araunah the Jebusite [2 Samuel 24:16].

In 1 Chronicles, the writer describes the angel David saw. This angel was sent to intervene for God. We see in this description another visual image which may be vividly remembered.

> David looked up and saw the angel of the Lord standing between heaven and earth with a drawn sword in his hand extended over Jerusalem... [1 Chronicles 21:16].

Hezekiah, King of Judah and all of Jerusalem were facing destruction by Sennecherib, the King of Assyria. Hezekiah prayed to the Lord and asked to be delivered from this king. The Assyrians were haughty and they reproached the Israelites. Isaiah prophesied their defeat.

> That night the angel of the Lord went out and put to death a hundred and eighty-five thousand men in the Assyrian camp. When the people got up the next morning—there were all the dead bodies! [2 Kings 19:35].

At a later time, the New Testament described a time when an angel interfered with the life of Herod on behalf of God. The angel was God's agent in the punishment of Herod. We are not told that the angel appeared to Herod, or that anyone else saw him. We do know that the angel struck Herod because Herod allowed the people to give him praise as if he were God.

> Immediately, because Herod did not give praise to God, an angel of the Lord struck him down, and he was eaten by worms and died [Acts 12:23].

These angels of God carried out God's judgment against His people and their enemies. Compare God's intervening angels with the characterization of a traditional angel that prevails in the world today.

GUIDING ANGELS

God sent angels to guide and instruct His people. When Abraham wanted a wife for Isaac, he sent his servant back to his homeland. He assured the servant of God's guidance by an angel.

> "The Lord, the God of heaven, who brought me out of my father's household and my native land and who

spoke to me and promised me on oath, saying, 'To your offspring I will give this land'— he will send his angel before you so that you can get a wife for my son from there" [Genesis 24:7].

Abraham's servant told Laban about the angel whom God had sent with him to aid him in getting a wife for Isaac.

He replied, "The Lord, before whom I have walked, will send his angel with you and make your journey a success, so that you can get a wife for my son from my own clan and from my father's family" [Genesis 24:40].

In their exodus from Egypt, the visible symbol of God's presence with His people was a pillar of cloud by day and a pillar of fire at night. This sign preceded them "to guide them on their way" [Exodus 13:21]. God's angel also accompanied the Israelites. God assured Moses of this angel's guidance.

My angel will go ahead of you and bring you into the land of Amorites, Hittites, Perizzites, Canaanites, Hivites and Jebusites, and I will wipe them out [Exodus 23:23].

When Moses went up on Mount Sinai, he stayed with God for forty days. The people became discouraged because they thought they were abandoned by Moses and by God. They persuaded Aaron to make a god to go before them. He made a golden calf from the articles of gold which they donated. After they bowed down and offered sacrifice to this idol, God still reassured Moses that He would continue to provide the angel to guide them.

Now go, lead the people to the place I spoke of, and my angel will go before you. However, when the time comes for me to punish, I will punish them for their sin [Exodus 32:34].

Moses wanted to lead Israel through the territory of Edom in peace. He sent a message to the King of Edom in which he outlined their circumstances and requested permission to travel through. In this message, Moses referred to the guiding angel,

. . .The Egyptians mistreated us and our fathers, but when we cried out to the Lord, he heard our cry and sent an angel and brought us out to Egypt. Now we are here at Kadesh, a town on the edge of your territory [Numbers 20:15b-16].

PROTECTING ANGELS

The protection of God's chosen people was one of the functions of the angels. The land which God intended to give to the Israelites was inhabited by six Canaanite nations. God temporarily withdrew His presence because of the sin of the people.

I will send an angel before you and drive out the Canaanites, Amorites, Hittites, Perizzites, Hivites and Jebusites. Go up to the land flowing with milk and honey. But I will not go with you, because you are a stiff-necked people and I might destroy you on the way [Exodus 33:2-3].

Moses, however was not satisfied with just an angel. Inasmuch as God was pleased with Moses, He consented to escort them. The same angel who guided Israel was also her protector.

A prayer of Isaiah recites the "kindness of the Lord." Isaiah details the saving of God's people from Egypt. He speaks of the angel of God who traveled with them and preserved and sheltered them.

In all their distress he too was distressed, and the angel of his presence saved them. In his love and mercy he redeemed them; he lifted them up and carried them all the days of old [Isaiah 63:9].

Three men of Judah, exiled in Babylon, refused to worship an image set by the king. They were punished by being put into a blazing furnace. In the furnace, the king saw a fourth man who "looked like a son of the gods." He perceived this to be a protecting angel.

Then Nebuchadnezzar said, "Praise be to the God of Shadrach, Meshach and Abednego, who has sent his angel and rescued his servants! They trusted in him and defied the king's command and were willing to give up their lives rather than serve or worship any god except their own God" [Daniel 3:28].

Later another king, Darius, was required, against his will, to punish Daniel when he disobeyed a royal decree by praying to God. News of Daniel's safety comforted the king.

"My God sent his angel, and he shut the mouths of the lions. They have not hurt me, because I was found innocent in his sight. Nor have I ever done any wrong before you, O king" [Daniel 6:22].

GUARDING ANGELS

God also provided angels to guard and defend His people. The angel who accompanied Israel from Egypt is represented as her guard, as well as her guide, and protector.

See, I am sending an angel ahead of you to guard you along the way and to bring you to the place I have prepared [Exodus 23:20].

When the Egyptians were pursuing the Israelites, the angel protected them by providing a rear guard to Israel.

Then the angel of God, who had been traveling in front of Israel's army, withdrew and went behind them. The pillar of cloud also moved from in front and stood behind them, [Exodus 14:19].

The psalmist, David, described the security guard which God supplied to Israel both individually and collectively.

The angel of the Lord encamps around those who fear him, and he delivers them [Psalm 34:7].

This is not a promise that God gives each person a guardian angel. This guarantee of safety was given to the chosen people who took refuge in God.

For he will command his angels concerning you to guard you in all your ways; they will lift you up in their hands, so that you will not strike your foot against a stone [Psalm 91:11-12].

Satan misused this passage when he tempted Jesus, telling Him to jump from the highest point of the Temple.

"If you are the Son of God," he said, "throw yourself down. For it is written: " 'He will command his angels concerning you, and they will lift you up in their hands, so that you will not strike your foot against a stone' " [Matthew 4:6]. Also see Luke 4:10-11.

The Book of Revelation describes "the Holy city, the New Jerusalem" (21:2). One of the functions of the angels is to guard the gates of this city of heaven.

It had a great, high wall with twelve gates, and with twelve angels at the gates. On the gates were written the names of the twelve tribes of Israel [Revelation 21:12].

MINISTERING ANGELS

Angels were sent by God to those who were in extreme need. They ministered to those who required sustenance and comfort, providing attention, food, encouragement, escape, and strength. In Hebrews, all angels are called "ministering spirits."

Are not all angels ministering spirits sent to serve those who will inherit salvation? [Hebrews 1:14].

Although this sounds like a question, it does not suggest that the writer questions the statement. In *A Commentary on the Epistle to the Hebrews*, Robert Milligan said this is a form of speech used to forcefully declare an unmistakable fact.

When Ishmael was about to die of thirst, the angel of God ministered to him and his mother, Hagar, in the desert.

God heard the boy crying, and the angel of God called to Hagar from heaven and said to her, "What is the matter, Hagar? Do not be afraid; God has heard the boy crying as he lies there. Lift the boy up and take him by the hand, for I will make him into a great nation" [Genesis 21:17-18].

Elijah was afraid for his life when he ran from Jezebel and hid in the desert. He was so depressed that he asked God to let him die. The angel ministered to the discouraged prophet before he began his forty day journey to Mount Horeb, without food.

> Then he lay down under the tree and fell asleep. All at once an angel touched him and said, "Get up and eat." . . . The angel of the Lord came back a second time and touched him and said, "Get up and eat, for the journey is too much for you" [1 Kings 19:5,7].

When Jesus was baptized by John, He went into the desert and fasted for forty days. After that Satan tempted Jesus, then angels attended Him.

> Then the devil left him, and angels came and attended him [Matthew 4:11].

> . . . and he was in the desert forty days, being tempted by Satan. He was with the wild animals, and angels attended him [Mark 1:13].

Luke does not tell us of the angels attending Jesus after the temptation, but only Luke, of the four Gospel writers, tells of the angel who encouraged Jesus just before Judas betrayed him.

> An angel from heaven appeared to him and strengthened him [Luke 22:43].

The apostles had been performing miracles and healing the sick, but the high priest and the Sadducees were jealous, and had them arrested. An angel ministered to the apostles by helping them to escape.

> But during the night an angel of the Lord opened the doors of the jail and brought them out [Acts 5:19].

About ten years after Jesus' death Herod had the apostle James arrested. James was the first apostle to die in the service of Jesus. Then Herod took Peter prisoner because he saw that the Jews were pleased by James' death. This occurred during the week-long celebration of Passover so that Peter was held in prison awaiting trial. Assembled at the home of Mark's mother, Mary, the church was earnestly praying for Peter. Although he was chained between two soldiers, and sentries guarded the entrance, Peter was helped to escape from prison by the ministry of an angel.

> Then Peter came to himself and said, "Now I know without a doubt that the Lord sent his angel and rescued me from Herod's clutches and from everything the Jewish people were anticipating" [Acts 12:11].

Paul was a prisoner aboard ship, traveling to Rome, when a violent storm arose. When he was about to be shipwrecked, Paul was reassured by the ministry of an angel.

> Last night an angel of the God whose I am and whom I serve stood beside me and said, "Do not be afraid, Paul. You must stand trial before Caesar, and God has graciously given you the lives of all who sail with you" [Acts 27:23-24].

INTERPRETING ANGELS

Angels not only delivered God's messages to His people, at times they interpreted the messages. Daniel was allowed to see visions which required some interpretation. He had a dream about four beasts which troubled him. He asked an angel the meaning of what he saw. He was given an explanation by the angel to allow him to understand God's message.

> I approached one of those standing there and asked him the true meaning of all this. So he told me and gave me the interpretation of these things: [Daniel 7:16].

Later, Daniel had a dream about a ram and a goat which he did not understand. The angel Gabriel was sent to him with an interpretation.

> And I heard a man's voice from the Ulai calling, "Gabriel, tell this man the meaning of the vision" [Daniel 8:16].

Hundreds of years later, as recorded in the New Testament, the same angel, Gabriel, brought God's messages to Zechariah and to Mary.

In the Old Testament, another man named Zechariah was a prophet who served God after the Jews returned from captivity. He was also a priest, and he wrote the Book of Zechariah. He was given eight prophetic visions which came to him in a single night. These visions were recorded in Zechariah 1:7 - 6:8. Throughout this passage there was an interpreting angel who was often called "the angel who was speaking to me," by Zechariah.

I asked, "What are these, my lord?" The angel who was talking with me answered, "I will show you what they are" [Zechariah 1:9].

I asked the angel who was speaking to me, "What are these?" He answered me, "These are the horns that scattered Judah, Israel and Jerusalem" [Zechariah 1:19].

The interpretation of a vision was also necessary to John in the Revelation. He saw many things which he did not understand. The explanation he required was provided by an interpreting angel.

Then the angel said to me: "Why are you astonished? I will explain to you the mystery of the woman and of the beast she rides, which has the seven heads and ten horns" [Revelation 17:7].

DELIVERY OF LAW BY ANGELS

In the Book of Exodus, we read that the law was given to Moses on Mount Sinai. There is no mention here of the involvement of angels in this transaction. We learn, however, from other Scripture references that angels were the agents of God in giving the law to Moses. Moses was the mediator between the angel and God's people.

In his speech before the Sanhedrin, Stephen refers to the angel who spoke to Moses on Mount Sinai.

He was in the assembly in the desert, with the angel who spoke to him on Mount Sinai, and with our fathers; and he received living words to pass on to us [Acts 7:38].

Later, in the same chapter, he speaks of the law being put into effect by angels:

And now you have betrayed and murdered him — you who have received the law that was put into effect through angels but have not obeyed it [Acts 7:52b-53].

It was traditional for the Jews at that time to believe that the law was given to Moses by angels, just as he was called to serve God by an angel. The implication here is that Stephen accepted that interpretation of the agency of angels in the giving of the law.

The law given to Moses at Sinai is called "the message spoken by angels" by the writer of Hebrews.

For if the message spoken by angels was binding, and every violation and disobedience received its just punishment, how shall we escape if we ignore such a great salvation? [Hebrews 2:2-3a].

Paul wrote to the Galatians of the law being "put into effect through angels," when he considered the law and the promise of Christ.

What, then, was the purpose of the law? It was added because of transgressions until the Seed to whom the promise referred had come. The law was put into effect through angels by a mediator [Galatians 3:19].

The mediator who is referred to in this verse is Moses, by whom the angels put the law into effect.

PRESENT PERFORMANCE OF ANGELS

Now we will think about the role which angels of God play in His service today. What is the capacity in which angels serve God at the present time? Is there any interaction between the angels and people on earth today? Angels were characters in many of the passages recorded for us in the Old Testament, the Gospels, and Acts. As the miraculous age came to a close, the record of the active participation of angels in the lives of men also ceased. It was an angel who brought John the Revelation, and many angels were seen by him as symbols in this prophecy. There is, however, no disclosure of the appearance of angels on earth after the time of the events related in the Book of Acts.

PRAISING ANGELS

One of the functions of the angels is the privilege to give praise to God. This call to praise God is given to them in the Psalms. The following verses give example of the angels call to praise God:

Praise the Lord, you his angels, you mighty ones who do his bidding, who obey his word. Praise the Lord, all his heavenly hosts, you his servants who do his will [Psalm 103:20-21].

Praise him, all his angels, praise him, all his heavenly hosts. . . .Let them praise the name of the Lord, for he commanded and they were created [Psalm 148:2,5].

As the Israelites praised, they acknowledged God's greatness, recognizing that the angels, or "multitudes of heaven" worship Him.

You alone are the Lord. You made the heavens, even the highest heavens, and all their starry host, the earth and all that is on it, the seas and all that is in them. You give life to everything, and the multitudes of heaven worship you [Nehemiah 9:6].

In this psalm of praise, David called all the angelic hosts to worship the Lord. The phrase "mighty ones" literally means "sons of God."

Ascribe to the Lord, O mighty ones, ascribe to the Lord glory and strength. Ascribe to the Lord the glory due his name; worship the Lord in the splendor of his holiness [Psalm 29:1-2].

ATTENDING ANGELS

The throne of God in heaven was described by the prophets of the Old Testament in a symbollic manner. They used the familiar earthly kings and their courts to tell about the heavenly realm.

> In the year that King Uzziah died, I saw the Lord seated on a throne, high and exalted, and the train of his robe filled the temple" [Isaiah 6:1].

> Micaiah continued, "Therefore hear the word of the Lord: I saw the Lord sitting on his throne with all the host of heaven standing around him on his right and on his left" [1 Kings 22:19].

This scene of God's throne pictured Him as surrounded by the angels, or "the host of heaven."

The psalmist pictured God and His angels meeting together in heaven in a council.

> The heavens praise your wonders, O Lord, your faithfulness too, in the assembly of the holy ones. For who in the skies above can compare with the Lord? Who is like the Lord among the heavenly beings? In the council of the holy ones God is greatly feared; he is more awesome than all who surround him [Psalm 89:5-7].

We learn from the Book of Job that the angels as well as Satan periodically assembled themselves in a heavenly council before the Lord.

> One day the angels came to present themselves before the Lord, and Satan also came with them [Job 1:6].

> On another day the angels came to present themselves before the Lord, and Satan also came with them to present himself before him [Job 2:1].

ACCOMPANYING ANGELS

We assume that angels will continue to escort the faithful to paradise as they did in the account of the rich man and Lazarus. This may be a parable, and therefore, symbolic. If so, it would be the only parable of Jesus in which a character was called by a proper name. Whether it is a parable, does not change the lesson or example which is taught. This story tells of the angels carrying

Lazarus to be with Abraham in paradise. The example is one of angels accompanying the dead.

> The time came when the beggar died and the angels carried him to Abraham's side. The rich man also died and was buried [Luke 16:22].

There is no reason to believe that angels are involved in any function with humans on earth today. There is no record of angelic appearances on earth during the time the Epistles were written. God discontinued His communication with man through the agency of angel messengers. We do not live in an age when God blesses and protects us by supernatural means.

When you ask in prayer for some favorable circumstance, do you pray for God to send His angels to grant your request? Do we expect that He will send His angels to us if we are in distress? If He does not send them, does this mean He no longer cares? Is He able to help and support us without using angels? As the Lord said to Moses, "Is the Lord's arm too short? . . ." [Numbers 11:23]. He is able to sustain and uphold us, but He no longer does it through use of His angels. It would be very difficult to specify any function of angels on earth today. If there is any capacity in which angels serve on earth today, it is not evident to us from a study of the Scriptures.

FUTURE PERFORMANCE OF ANGELS

Finally, we will consider the operations in which the angels will be involved in the future. At the end of the present age, when Jesus returns "in his glory," He will be accompanied and assisted by angels. He will also acknowledge and confess us before God if we have acknowledged and confessed Him before men.

WITNESSING ANGELS

In sending out His twelve apostles, one of the things Jesus taught was that men should confess Him to be the Son of God. Matthew records Jesus saying He would recognize before God those who confess Him, and disown before God anyone who disowned him.

Whoever acknowledges me before men, I will also acknowledge him before my Father in heaven. But whoever disowns me before men, I will disown him before my Father in heaven [Matthew 10:32-33].

Luke stated further that this recognition or rejection will be before the angels.

I tell you, whoever acknowledges me before men, the Son of Man will also acknowledge him before the angels of God. But he who disowns me before men will be disowned before the angels of God [Luke 12:8-9].

Earlier Luke had recorded Jesus' admonition not to be ashamed of Him or His words. If we are ashamed of Him, He will be ashamed of us when He comes again with the angels.

If anyone is ashamed of me and my words, the Son of Man will be ashamed of him when he comes in his glory and in the glory of the Father and of the holy angels [Luke 9:26].

ASSISTING ANGELS

At some unknown time in the future, the angels will have specific duties associated with the return of Christ and the judgment. These verses refer to that time when the Lord will come again. The angels will participate as He returns surrounded by the brightness of God.

For the Son of Man is going to come in his Father's glory with his angels, and then he will reward each person according to what he has done [Matthew 16:27].

The Lord will reward people in accordance with the lives they lived on earth.

When Christ Jesus reappears, He will be joined by angels. The archangel will give a resounding order as he accompanies them.

When the Son of Man comes in his glory, and all the angels with him, he will sit on his throne in heavenly glory [Matthew 25:31].

For the Lord himself will come down from heaven, with a loud command, with the voice of the archangel and with the trumpet call of God, and the dead in Christ will rise first [1 Thessalonians 4:16].

...This will happen when the Lord Jesus is revealed from heaven in blazing fire with his powerful angels [2 Thessalonians 1:7].

In preparation for the time of judgment, the angels will first gather the saints of God together. Both the parable of the sower and the parable of the net teach that the angels will be employed in the final separation of the righteous and the wicked.

And he will send his angels with a loud trumpet call, and they will gather his elect from the four winds, from one end of the heavens to the other [Matthew 24:31].

...The harvest is the end of the age, and the harvesters are angels. As the weeds are pulled up and burned in the fire, so it will be at the end of the age. The Son of Man will send out his angels, and they will weed out of his kingdom everything that causes sin and all who do evil. They will throw them into the fiery furnace, where there will be weeping and gnashing of teeth [Matthew 13:39b-42].

This is how it will be at the end of the age. The angels will come and separate the wicked from the righteous and throw them into the fiery furnace, where there will be weeping and gnashing of teeth [Matthew 13:49-50].

SUMMARY

Although the Bible does not list the functions of the angels, we can learn some of their duties from various references. One of the responsibilities of angels was to deliver God's messages. Hagar, Manoah's wife, Zechariah, and Mary each received a message from an angel that they would have a child. The shepherds received the announcement message of Jesus' birth from an angel. Lot, the Wise Men and Joseph also received communication from angels.

Dispensing God's providence was another function of the angels. God intervened in people's lives by the use of angels. This resulted in the loss of many lives as angels executed God's verdict on people.

An angel was charged with guiding Abraham's servant to find Isaac's wife. The angel preceded the Israelites in the exodus from Egypt. This angel was responsible for their protection against enemies. Angels guarded and defended God's people and they guard the gates of heaven.

Angels ministered to many people who were in distress. The angel of the Lord was responsible for preserving the lives of Ishmael, Hagar, and Elijah. Jesus was attended by angels after His temptation. He was also strengthened by an angel before He was arrested. The apostles were freed from jail and later Peter was helped to escape from prison by angels. Paul was sustained during a storm at sea by the ministry of an angel.

Angels were interpreters of visions and dreams. Messages were interpreted for Daniel, Zechariah, and John by angels. The angels were involved in some way in the delivery of the law to Moses. Angels give praise to God and worship Him. They are attendants who are present at His throne. They witness confessions and escort the dead to await judgment. Angels will attend Christ when He returns. They will aid in gathering the saints and separating the righteous from the wicked.

There is no reason to believe that angels are involved in any function with man on earth today. The record of appearances to men ended with the events in the Book of Acts.

REVIEW

1. Name some people who received messages from God through angels. _____

   _____

2. How did angels intervene on behalf of God?____

   _____

   _____

3. Name three ways angels served to preserve God's people. _____

_____

4. Name five people who received the ministry of angels.

_____

5. Who received interpretation of God's message from angels? _____

_____

6. What was the role of angels concerning the law of Moses? _____

_____

7. What function of angels do we learn from the story of the rich man and Lazarus? _____

_____

8. When was the last recorded appearance of an angel on earth? _____

9. What will be the work of angels at the resurrection?

_____

10. What is the role of angels with man today?____

_____

NOTES

_____
_____
_____
_____
_____
_____
_____
_____
_____
_____
_____
_____

Chapter Three

Reported Sightings

I t is not at all unusual today to hear of the reported sighting of an unidentified flying object. Many people insist on revealing their adventures with aliens from another planet. When these accounts are investigated, the events are usually proven to be a hoax or a misrepresentation of facts. Most of us find these things ridiculous.

The books of both the Old and New Testaments reported occasions when people saw angels. These are infallible reports which were recorded by inspired writers. Because of our faith in God and the trust we place in His Word, we believe these accounts to be truth.

The age of the miraculous has ended and God no longer uses angels in His dealings with mankind. In the same way that some continue to report miracles of healing and meetings with aliens, people are still publicizing their experiences with angels.

It was not uncommon in the centuries which followed the supernatural age of the New Testament for humans to report the visit of an angel. By the time of the Middle Ages, it was considered logical and reasonable for a person to expect to encounter an angel in his lifetime. Thus, any experience which seemed unexplainable was likely to be justified as the operation of an angel. When we combine this type of information with folklore, the result is an excessive amount of data which had nothing to do with the Scriptures. From this abundance, many have acquired their knowledge of angels.

DESCRIPTION

We have already learned that the Bible is not specific in describing the likeness of an angel. Therefore, we wonder what the face of Stephen looked like when he appeared before the Sanhedrin.

> All who were sitting in the Sanhedrin looked intently at Stephen, and they saw that his face was like the face of an angel [Acts 6:15].

What did these people see in Stephen's face? Whatever the quality was, Luke says they identified it with an angel. Was it a look of courage, serenity, or did his face appear to glow or radiate with brightness? What caused those who saw him to equate the appearance of Stephen's face with that of an angel?

Angels are spirits, and as such, they do not have a material body or form as we do. Angels often took the form of men when they appeared on earth. Mistakenly, many have begun to think of them as spiritual beings inhabiting physical bodies.

There is no particular verse in the Bible which says, "This is what an angel looks like." There is no person alive to whom we can turn for this information. It is safe to say that God alone knows the look or the image of an angel. We can, however, learn much from what He has revealed to us in the Scripture.

The justification for our belief in the existence and operation of angels is not based entirely on the verses of Scripture which acquaint us with their appearances on earth in physical bodies. We believe that the angels are spirits who reside in heaven with God, and that He used them in a supernatural way to communicate with mankind.

We feel compelled to continue to search for a description of an angel. Therefore, we begin by examining a number of Scripture references, remembering that these verses describe angels who took on a form in order to be seen by mortal beings and understood by human minds.

OLD TESTAMENT DESCRIPTIONS

There is no record of an angel appearing to a human being before the time of Abraham. Angels in the Old

Testament were never described in great detail. When they appeared as men, we are not given a specific account. Their shape, manner, or clothing was not even mentioned. At times an angel was simply called "a man," at other times just "an angel," or "the angel of the Lord." Apparently, there were times when there was nothing unusual in their outward appearance. These beings must have seemed to be quite ordinary on these occasions, because often they were not recognized to be anything other than men.

At other times, angels took forms other than the bodies of men. God is said by the Psalmist, to use winds and flames of fire as His messengers and His servants.

> He makes winds his messengers, flames of fire his servants [Psalm 104:4].

Later, the New Testament writer of the letter to the Hebrews told us that this was a reference to the angels. God employed His angels as messengers and servants in some ways which were different from their coming down to earth to make appearances in the bodies of men.

> In speaking of the angels he says, "He makes his angels winds, his servants flames of fire" [Hebrews 1:7].

There is another passage which describes the appearance of an angel in flames. It is an occasion in the life of Moses when God called him to lead His people out of the slavery of the Egyptians.

> There the angel of the Lord appeared to him in flames of fire from within a bush. Moses saw that though the bush was on fire it did not burn up" [Exodus 3:2].

In the entire Old Testament, representing a period of over a thousand years, angelic appearances were recorded only nineteen times. The majority of the prophets of God, especially those who wrote before the Exile, had little to say about angels. In later writings of the prophets, there is increased reference to the angels. The effect brought about by the course of history has a direct relation to the changes in Jewish beliefs concerning angels. When these people were taken from their own land and forced to live in exile among pagan races, the assimilation of knowledge relating to spirit beliefs altered their perception of God's angels.

Daniel provided us with a great deal of information for the study of angels. He presented the fourth man in the fiery furnace who was presumed by the king to be an angel (3:25-28). Another angel who played a significant role in The Book of Daniel was the angel who saved Daniel from the lions (6:22). Daniel is the only Old Testament writer who gave angels personality and called them by proper names. He is the first to tell us of the angels Michael and Gabriel.

In the book of Zechariah, angels were present almost continuously. The book contains a number of symbollic visions which are explained to the prophet by an angel. Other angels appear throughout the writing.

INVISIBLE ANGEL

Angels had the ability to assume any disguise or cover, any shape or form which was consistent with the purpose of their appearing. The angel of the Lord was, on one occasion, invisible to the human eye, but later became visible.

When Balaam, the pagan prophet of Moab, was displeasing to God, the angel of the Lord stood in his path. At first, only Balaam's donkey saw the angel. Later the angel was revealed to Balaam as well.

Then the Lord opened Balaam's eyes, and he saw the angel of the Lord standing in the road with his sword drawn. So he bowed low and fell facedown [Numbers 22:31].

NEW TESTAMENT DESCRIPTIONS

When the Jews were exposed to Babylonian and Persian religions during the Exile, one result was a change in their concept of the spirit world, including angels. The oppression of the Jews and their experience with the culture and tradition of a society dominated by Near Eastern influence are responsible for shaping the world in which the Christian era began.

In the New Testament when angels appeared on earth as men, they were described in greater detail. These appearances were also recorded more frequently in the New Testament. In approximately one hundred years spanned by the New Testament, angelic appearances were recorded thirteen times. The angels who appeared to people in the New Testament were portrayed in a more specific manner than those in the Old Testament.

Often some description of their garments was given. We specifically observe the mention of white clothing and the brightness of lightning. Consider these accounts from the four Gospels of the angels at the tomb of Jesus:

His appearance was like lightning, and his clothes were white as snow [Matthew 28:3].

. . . a young man dressed in a white robe. . .[Mark 16:5].

. . . two men in clothes that gleamed like lightning. . .[Luke 24:4].

. . . two angels in white, . . . one at the head and the other at the foot [John 20:12].

At the ascension of Christ, the beings who appeared were described in a similar manner. We believe these were angels and they were simply described as:

. . . two men dressed in white. . ." [Acts 1:10].

Cornelius had a vision in which he saw an angel. It was this angel who instructed him to send for Peter. When Peter questioned him, Cornelius told him about the angel whom he described as,

. . . a man in shining clothes. . . [Acts 10:30].

NAMES OF ANGELS

There is some indication that the angels who appeared to men were secretive about their names. At least, we have instances when they were asked and did not reveal their names.

Jacob struggled with a man whom Hosea tells us was God in the form of an angel (Hosea 12:3,4).

Jacob said, "Please tell me your name."

But he replied, "Why do you ask my name?" Then he blessed him there [Genesis 32:29].

The angel of the Lord visited Manoah and his wife to inform them that they would become the parents of Samson. Manoah wanted to know the identity of this angel.

Then Manoah inquired of the angel of the Lord, "What is your name, so that we may honor you when your word comes true?"

He replied, "Why do you ask my name? It is beyond understanding" [Judges 13:17-18].

The King James Version translates the phrase "it is secret," and the American Standard Version says "it is wonderful."

Thus we see that at times the messenger did not want to identify himself by name. Most often, the angel's name was not given, even if requested. Perhaps too much emphasis on the carrier could detract from the message. It is signficant that in the hundreds of verses of scriptural reference to angels, only two, Michael and Gabriel, are identified by name.

FRIGHTENING ANGELS

There was something very frightening about the appearance of an angel. Notice, in the following references, frequently the angel said, "Do not be afraid." Often those who were privileged to see the appearance of an angel were absolutely terrified.

Maybe this was because the angel suddenly or unexpectedly became visible and the surprise shocked or alarmed the person. Or perhaps the brightness, which is often mentioned was dazzling to those who witnessed the appearance.

God told Moses that anyone who looked at His face would not be allowed to live.

"But," he said, "you cannot see my face, for no one may see me and live" [Exodus 33:20].

In ancient times, the Jews believed that looking at an angel, the agent of God, face to face also meant certain death. This explains Gideon's fear and the need for the reassurance given to him by the angel.

> When Gideon realized that it was the angel of the Lord, he exclaimed, "Ah, Sovereign Lord! I have seen the angel of the Lord face to face!"
> But the Lord said to him, "Peace! Do not be afraid. You are not going to die" [Judges 6:22-23].

The traditionally accepted belief, that seeing an angel would cause immediate death, was apparently believed by Manoah and his wife. They thought they would die after seeing the angel of the Lord.

> When the angel of the Lord did not show himself again to Manoah and his wife, Manoah realized that it was the angel of the Lord.
> "We are doomed to die!" he said to his wife. "We have seen God!" [Judges 13:21-22].

Daniel was also frightened when he looked at the angel. The angel Gabriel came to him. Daniel was speaking of Gabriel when he said:

> As he came near the place where I was standing, I was terrified and fell prostrate. . .[Daniel 8:17a].

It was also common in New Testament times to react to an angelic appearance with fear. Often the angel who appeared, gave reassurance to people by saying: "Do not be afraid." One of these occasions was when Zechariah, the father of John the Baptist, was surprised by the angel in the temple. It is certain that he was startled, but he was also terribly frightened.

> When Zechariah saw him, he was startled and was gripped with fear. But the angel said to him: "Do not be afraid, Zechariah; your prayer has been heard. Your wife Elizabeth will bear you a son, and you are to give him the name John" [Luke 1:12-13].

Another frightening experience was Mary's visit from the angel Gabriel. Possibly Mary was more disturbed by the angel's greeting than by his appearance. Since she was disturbed by the content of his message, this may have been more frightening than his actual appearance.

The angel went to her and said, "Greetings, you who are highly favored! The Lord is with you."

Mary was greatly troubled at his words and wondered what kind of greeting this might be. But the angel said to her, "Do not be afraid, Mary, you have found favor with God" [Luke 1:28-30].

When we think of the shepherds at the time of Jesus' birth, we are more likely to emphasize the joy and privilege they experienced than the fear. We realize that they were common people engaged in a humble occupation, and yet, they were chosen by God to receive the message of the birth of God's only Son. The shepherds who saw the angel appear, with the glory of the Lord shining around him, and heard his significant message were "terrified."

An angel of the Lord appeared to them, and the glory of the Lord shone around them, and they were terrified. But the angel said to them, "Do not be afraid. I bring you good news of great joy that willl be for all the people" [Luke 2:9-10].

At the tomb of Jesus, the angel told the women who saw him, not to be alarmed. In spite of the angel's attempt to relieve their distress, they were demonstrating the panic they experienced by shaking with fear.

Trembling and bewildered, the women went out and fled from the tomb. They said nothing to anyone, because they were afraid [Mark 16:8].

Not only the women who went to the tomb to prepare Jesus' body were frightened; the Roman soldiers sent by Pilate to guard the tomb also trembled with fright.

There was a violent earthquake, for an angel of the Lord came down from heaven and, going to the tomb, rolled back the stone and sat on it. His appearance was like lightning, and his clothes were white as snow. The guards were so afraid of him that they shook and became like dead men [Matthew 28:2-4].

REVELATION ANGELS

The Book of Revelation is John's description of his vision. The angels revealed to him in this vision were symbolic and his descriptions should not be taken as literal depictions of the angels of heaven.

And I saw a mighty angel proclaiming in a loud voice, "Who is worthy to break the seals and open the scroll?" [Revelation 5:2].

Then I saw another mighty angel coming down from heaven. He was robed in a cloud, with a rainbow above his head; his face was like the sun, and his legs were like fiery pillars. He was holding a little scroll, which lay open in his hand. He planted his right foot on the sea and his left foot on the land, and he gave a loud shout like the roar of a lion. When he shouted, the voices of the seven thunders spoke [Revelation 10:1-3].

Out of the temple came the seven angels with the seven plagues. They were dressed in clean, shining linen and wore golden sashes around their chests [Revelation 15:6].

After this I saw another angel coming down from heaven. He had great authority, and the earth was illuminated by his splendor [Revelation 18:1].

The word angel is used more than seventy times in the book of Revelation. In addition, there are also references to heavenly hosts, holy ones, and the angels Gabriel and Michael, who are mentioned by name.

ANGELS APPEARING WITH JESUS?

During Jesus' ministry, there is no account of an angelic appearance to anyone who was in His presence. It is not recorded in the Scripture that a messenger from God appeared to a human being when His Son was present.

Angels were in the presence of Jesus while He was here on earth at least twice. Matthew and Mark tell us that He was attended by angels after the temptation by the devil. Luke set down the account of an angel who came and strengthened Him before He was betrayed. There is, however, no record of any angel appearing to a human being or speaking to any person who was in the presence of Jesus. It was unnecessary for God to communicate with men through the agency of angels when they were in the company of His Son.

ANGELS APPEARING TODAY?

Following the Book of Acts, the Bible does not give an account of any appearance of angels to a person on earth. We may assume that these appearances ceased at that time. We have no reason to believe that God sends angels to appear on earth today.

In the supernatural age, God used miraculous measures. He communicated with humanity by means of angel messengers. We have His message to us in the form of the Written Word. He no longer sends His angels to bring messages to people. There is no need for the miraculous appearance of angels in the present age. The use of angels as messengers ended when the age of miracles closed. This does not mean that God's concern for us is less than with the people of long ago. He is able to care for us in any way that He desires.

Angels were never sent to preach the Gospel nor will they be allowed to preach any other gospel. The appearance of an angel for the purpose of preaching a different gospel was specifically condemned by Paul's letter to the Galatians.

> But even if we or an angel from heaven should preach a gospel other than the one we preached to you, let him be eternally condemned! [Galatians 1:8].

SUMMARY

Although a detailed description of angels in heaven is not given, the mental image of an angel as a winged, human figure is not supported by Scripture. We learn from biblical records of their earthly appearances that angels sometimes assumed human bodies. They are, however, spiritual in nature and substance as well. Their home is heaven which is not a place of flesh and blood bodies

(1 Corinthians 15:35-49). At times, angels were invisible to the human eye, but later became visible.

The Old Testament is much more conservative in its descriptive information than the New Testament. The majority of the prophets do not contribute any information concerning the angels. Angelic appearances very often frightened people. Some aspect of seeing an angel filled a person with absolute terror. The Book of Revelation has numerous references to angels seen by John in a vision.

There is no record of angelic appearances to people who were in the presence of Jesus. There is no record, in Scripture, of earthly appearances of angels after the events recorded in the Book of Acts. There is no reason to believe that angels appear on earth today.

REVIEW

1. How does Luke describe the face of Stephen?

   _____

2. Describe an angel. _____

   _____

3. Which records more frequent appearances of angels, the Old Testament or the New Testament? _____

4. Name two prophets who wrote concerning angels.

   _____

5. With regard to angels, what difference is notable in the writing of the New Testament? _____

   _____

   _____

6. Name possible causes of the fear produced by the appearance of an angel. _____

   _____

   _____

7. What book in the New Testament mentions angels most often? _____

   _____

8. Did angels ever appear to people when Jesus was present?_____

9 . Do angels appear to people in the world today? If so, for what purpose? _____

_____

NOTES

_____
_____
_____
_____
_____
_____
_____
_____
_____
_____
_____
_____
_____
_____
_____
_____
_____
_____
_____
_____
_____
_____
_____
_____
_____
_____
_____
_____
_____
_____

Chapter Four

Organization Chart

RANKING OF ANGELS

The Bible does not set forth a detailed classification and ranking of the angels in heaven. They are sometimes called by names other than "angel," but this is not done in a manner that would assign rank. Some of these names are: heavenly beings, heavenly hosts, holy ones, hosts of heaven, multitudes of heaven, and mighty ones.

Paul wrote to Timothy of particular angels selected to oversee interactions of the church, along with God and Christ.

> I charge you in the sight of God and Christ Jesus and the elect angels, to keep these instructions without partiality, and to do nothing out of favoritism [1 Timothy 5:21].

The Bible also names other celestial beings: cherubim, seraphim, and living creatures. We have always been taught that these beings were kinds of angels, but they do not belong on our organization chart at all. One reason for our confusion of the subject is the tendency to group all heavenly creatures under the heading "ANGELS." For the purposes of our study, the cherubim, seraphim, and living creatures do not qualify as angels. They are not classes, or orders, or levels of angels, but heavenly beings in addition to angels.

ANGELS

Webster defines *angel* as: "a spiritual being superior to man in power and intelligence; literally, a messenger." This is an acceptable definition, but it continues, "one in the lowest rank of the Dionysian hierarchy." This definition is unacceptable, since the work of Dionysius cannot be substantiated by Scripture.

Dionysius was converted by Paul as recorded in Acts 17:34. He was a member of the Areopagus, an aristocratic council of ancient Athens. This man was supposed to have written several important theological letters and books. One of these was "The Celestial Hierarchy." This literature received a position of great authority because it was attributed to a follower of Paul and it was believed that Paul provided the information which he received by divine revelation at the time of his vision of paradise (2 Corinthians 12:2-7).

The writings were translated from Greek to Latin in the 9th century and many commentaries were written to examine and give honor to the work. For a period of more than 1,000 years, these writings were considered to be genuine and authoritative.

Since that time, scholars have discovered the writing to be the work of an unknown Syrian theologian who lived about 500 A.D. There has been an extensive investigation to determine the identity of the Greek author who preferred to distribute his writing under the name Dionysius the Areopagite. The untruthful use of the author's name is so widely accepted today that he is now called Pseudo-Dionysius (False-Dionysius).

In "The Celestial Hierarchy," Pseudo-Dionysius named the levels of angels, which he ranked from highest to lowest in nine orders. They are: Seraphim, Cherubim, Thrones, Dominions, Authorities, Powers, Principalities, Archangels, and Angels. He was not the first to teach this scheme, but his work became the basis for all subsequent speculation. In the sixteenth century his writings were placed on a level almost equal with the Gospels, but the work of Pseudo-Dionysius is no longer considered authoritative.

The angels of God are a group of spirit beings, created before the creation of the earth to be representatives, messengers, or agents of God in his dealings with man. The Bible does not grade angels in order of excellence or importance. The position of angels is higher than man and lower than Christ. Quoting David, from Psalm 8, the writer of Hebrews, speaking of Christ said:

So he became as much superior to the angels as the name he has inherited is superior to theirs. For to which of the angels did God ever say, "You are my Son; today I have become your Father" [Hebrews 1:4-5].

ARCHANGEL

The Bible assigned a superior position to only one angel, who was called the archangel. In addition to his rank of archangel, he was also a military commander of a group of angels.

And there was war in heaven. Michael and his angels fought against the dragon, and the dragon and his angels fought back [Revelation 12:7].

The prefix "arch" means "chief or highest," so the word "archangel," from the Greek word *archangelos*, means the chief angel or the highest angel. The word "archangel" does not appear in the Old Testament, and is found only twice in the New Testament—1 Thessalonians 4:16 and Jude 9.

For the Lord himself will come down from heaven, with a loud command, with the voice of the archangel and with the trumpet call of God, and the dead in Christ will rise first [1 Thessalonians 4:16].

But even the archangel Michael, when he was disputing with the devil about the body of Moses, did not dare to bring a slanderous accusation against him, but said, "The Lord rebuke you!" [Jude verse 9].

Because a higher rank is given to one angel, some have created a complex system of grades, ranks or levels of angels which cannot be supported by Scripture. A great effort has been made over the centuries to disprove a single angel occupies the position of archangel. The word "archangel" is defined by Britannica as "any of several chiefs, rulers, or princes of angels."

One argument which many give to support this position is that in the original Greek, 1 Thessalonians 4:16 does not specify "the archangel." Instead, the wording is "a voice of an archangel." To some people this seems to be evidence that other archangels exist. It is true that there may be a plurality of archangels in the service of God, but in the Bible, this title is only given to one particular angel. In fact, the word archangel never appears in plural form in the entire Bible.

Since the phrase "one of the chief princes" is used in Daniel 10:13, some assume that if the angel is one of multiple chief princes, he is one of multiple archangels.

> But the prince of the Persian kingdom resisted me twenty-one days. Then Michael, one of the chief princes, came to help me, because I was detained there with the king of Persia [Daniel 10:13].

If we try to support the theory of a plurality of archangels, we are able to find some passages of Scripture in the symbolic language of the Book of Revelation which refer to seven angels who are grouped together in an unusual way. There is the implication that the angels who are in the direct company of God are in an exalted rank.

> John, to the seven churches in the province of Asia: Grace and peace to you from him who is, and who was, and who is to come, and from the seven spirits before his throne [Revelation 1:4].

> And I saw the seven angels who stand before God, and to them were given seven trumpets [Revelation 8:2].

> Out of the temple came the seven angels with the seven plagues. They were dressed in clean, shining linen and wore golden sashes around their chests [Revelation 15:6].

Numerous times these seven angels are mentioned individually as well as collectively in various other passages throughout the Book of Revelation.

MICHAEL

The study of Scripture reveals that only one angel, Michael, was called archangel. Webster, however, says that Michael is, "one of the four archangels named in Hebrew tradition." The name *Michael* means "he who is like God." Michael is introduced in the Book of Daniel, where he is called "one of the chief princes," and "the great prince who protects the people of God."

Jewish tradition expanded the role of Michael beyond the teaching of Scripture. Reference found in the Dead Sea Scrolls indicates a belief that at the Messiah's coming, Michael would be a pre-eminent character. Others believe that before Jesus was born to Mary, He existed as the angel Michael, and that at His ascension Jesus returned to heaven and resumed the identity of Michael. These notions about Michael are not found in Scripture.

In the third year of the reign of Cyrus of Persia, Daniel received a vision to aid his understanding of God's message. An angel was sent to explain the vision. The angel was unable to come to Daniel for three weeks because of interference from a Persian enemy. This resistance came from an apparent demon which controlled or at least had influence over the Persian realm. It was "Michael, one of the chief princes," who helped this angel, enabling him to come to Daniel. Michael was the only one who helped him.

But the prince of the Persian kingdom resisted me twenty-one days. Then Michael, one of the chief princes, came to help me, because I was detained there with the king of Persia [Daniel 10:13].

So he said, "Do you know why I have come to you? Soon I will return to fight against the prince of Persia, and when I go the prince of Greece will come; but first I will tell you what is written in the Book of Truth. No one supports me against them except Michael, your prince [Daniel 10:20-21].

At that time Michael, the great prince who protects your people, will arise. There will be a time of distress such as has not happened from the beginning of nations until then. But at that time your people—

everyone whose name is found written in the book —
will be delivered [Daniel 12:1].

The angel who spoke to Daniel referred to Michael as,
"your prince" (10:21). Later the angel told Daniel that
Michael was the protector of God's people. When these
phrases are considered together with "the prince of Persia"
and "the prince of Greece," we see Michael, "the great
prince," as a defender of Israel. The mythology of Canaan
was a belief in many gods and taught that each nation was
under the protection of one individual god.

Jewish tradition adapted this view of national guardians.
The Jews were absolutely monotheistic and they retained
their belief in one God by modifying the protectors of
nations to guardian angels instead of multiple gods.
According to Jewish belief, Michael was the guardian
angel of Israel and the greatest of all angels.

Those who accept the theory of multiple archangels
believe Michael to be the highest or chief archangel.
Although Jewish custom granted Michael an exaggerated
position, there is, nevertheless, only one archangel ever
mentioned in Scripture, and that of course is Michael.

Michael had the authority to contend with Satan over
the body of Moses. Although we are not certain why
Michael contested with Satan for Moses' body, we learn
more about Michael from this verse.

> But even the archangel Michael, when he was
> disputing with the devil about the body of Moses, did
> not dare to bring a slanderous accusation against him,
> but said, "The Lord rebuke you!" [Jude verse 9].

Origen was a Christian philosopher who lived and wrote
in the third century. He and others believed that this was
a reference to an apocryphal book, The Assumption of
Moses. The existing copies of this book, however, are no
longer available in complete form and do not contain
reference to this occurrence.

In the Book of Revelation, Michael is represented as a
military chief in the war between God and paganism. The
evil influence of idolatrous pagans is symbolized by the
dragon, Satan. Michael is pictured as the leader of a group
of angels who are warriors opposing the dragon.

> And there was war in heaven. Michael and his angels fought against the dragon, and the dragon and his angels fought back [Revelation 12:7].

Michael is presented by Scripture as an angel who works in behalf of the faithful. Although more is written in Scripture about Gabriel, only Michael is given the higher position of archangel.

GABRIEL

> The angel answered, "I am Gabriel. I stand in the presence of God, and I have been sent to speak to you and to tell you this good news" [Luke 1:19].

Gabriel is simply called an angel, but he is one of the angels who stands in the presence of God. Does this qualify him as an archangel? Gabriel is never given the title of archangel anywhere in the Bible.

The name *Gabriel* means "man of God." Gabriel first appeared in the Book of Daniel. On two occasions, when the prophet Daniel received visions, Gabriel was sent to tell him their meaning.

> And I heard a man's voice from the Ulai calling, "Gabriel, tell this man the meaning of the vision." As he came near the place where I was standing, I was terrified and fell prostrate. "Son of man," he said to me, "understand that the vision concerns the time of the end." While he was speaking to me, I was in a deep sleep, with my face to the ground. Then he touched me and raised me to my feet [Daniel 8:16-18].

> . . .while I was still in prayer, Gabriel, the man I had seen in the earlier vision, came to me in swift flight about the time of the evening sacrifice. He instructed me and said to me, "Daniel, I have now come to give you insight and understanding. As soon as you began to pray, an answer was given, which I have come to tell you, for you are highly esteemed. Therefore, consider the message and understand the vision" [Daniel 9:21-23].

Hundreds of years later, the New Testament record shows this same angel, Gabriel, was sent to Zechariah to foretell the birth of his son, John.

Then an angel of the Lord appeared to him, standing at the right side of the altar of incense. When Zechariah saw him, he was startled and was gripped with fear. But the angel said to him: "Do not be afraid, Zechariah; your prayer has been heard. Your wife Elizabeth will bear you a son, and you are to give him the name John" [Luke 1:11-13].

Zechariah did not readily accept Gabriel's prophecy, and because Zechariah did not believe him, Gabriel made Zechariah unable to speak. Zechariah remained mute until eight days after his son was born.

Zechariah asked the angel, "How can I be sure of this, I am an old man and my wife is well along in years."

The angel answered, "I am Gabriel. I stand in the presence of God, and I have been sent to speak to you and to tell you this good news. And now you will be silent and not able to speak until the day this happens, because you did not believe my words, which will come true at their proper time" [Luke 1:18-20].

Upon being questioned, Gabriel cited his credentials to Zechariah. "I am Gabriel. I stand in the presence of God." From this bit of information and the exaggeration of angelology in Jewish belief, Gabriel became one of four archangels, later seven, and then twelve.

Gabriel was also sent to Mary, with a very special message. He was sent to tell her that she would be the mother of a Son, whom she would name Jesus.

In the sixth month, God sent the angel Gabriel to Nazareth, a town in Galilee, to a virgin pledged to be married to a man named Joseph, a descendant of David. The virgin's name was Mary. The angel went to her and said, "Greetings, you who are highly favored! The Lord is with you."

Mary was greatly troubled at his words and wondered what kind of greeting this might be. But the angel said to her, "Do not be afraid, Mary, you have found favor with God. You will be with child and give birth to a son, and you are to give him the name Jesus" [Luke 1:26-31].

Gabriel is often given credit for appearances to Joseph, once before the birth of Jesus, again when he was warned to escape to Egypt, and also after Herod's death. This angel, however, was anonymous. He was never called by name and should not be confused with Gabriel (Matthew 1:20-24; 2:13,19).

Gabriel has, by tradition, been awarded the task of sounding "the trumpet call of God" (1 Thessalonians 4:16) at the time of the Lord's coming. This is associated with the multiple archangel theory. The verse says "with the voice of the archangel and with the trumpet call of God." There is no dispute that the voice of the archangel refers to Michael. Thus it seemed fitting to tradition that Gabriel be the one to sound the trumpet. This was made memorable by the song lyric "Gabriel, blow your horn." Paul, however, did not write to the Thessalonians that Gabriel will blow the trumpet, nor is it revealed anywhere in Scripture.

Though Gabriel and Michael are the only angels named in Scripture, the Apocryphal books name two more. The Book of Tobit introduces Raphael, and 2 Esdras identifies Uriel.

HIERARCHIES

Following the Exile and their exposure to the Babylonians and the Persians, the Jews created whole hierarchies of intermediary beings. A hierarchy is a body which is organized into orders or ranks in which each one is subordinate to the one above it. In order to support their theory of a hierarchy of angels, certain people have taken a text from Colossians to serve as evidence that the Bible teaches of various orders or classes of angels.

> He is the image of the invisible God, the firstborn over all creation. For by him all things were created: things in heaven and on earth, visible and invisible, whether thrones or powers or rulers or authorities; all things were created by him and for him [Colossians 1:15-16].

Paul was not furnishing us with a listing of the ranks of heavenly beings. He was writing to a group of people who were confused concerning the role of angels. They were so confused that they even worshipped angels. They had begun to use these ranks and divisions in reference to God's messengers. Paul was teaching the superiority of Christ to these Colossians who worshiped angels. He declared that all things were created by Christ and classified "things in heaven and on earth." He went on to say, "visible and invisible," and then he even included the names they used, thrones, powers, rulers, and authorities.

Another passage of Scripture which is quoted as an indication of a range of diverse ranks or levels of angels is found in Paul's letter to the Ephesians.

> . . .That power is like the working of his mighty strength, which he exerted in Christ when he raised him from the dead and seated him at his right hand in the heavenly realms, far above all rule and authority, power and dominion, and every title that can be given, not only in the present age but also in the one to come [Ephesians 1:19b-21].

According to several early Christian historians, the philosophy of false teachers was at work here in Ephesus. They were instructing their followers in the names which man had assigned to the varied classes of angels. So Paul used these names as he showed that all creatures, whatever mankind chooses to call them, are subject to the authority of Jesus.

CHERUBIM

Although the cherubim are not ordinary angels, we shall consider what the Bible teaches concerning these heavenly creatures. The word *cherubim* is plural. A Hebrew noun, in the masculine gender, ending in *im* is plural. The singular form of the word is *cherub*. The King James Version is repetitious in the use of the from *cherubims*.

The cherubim are the first of the heavenly beings to be specifically mentioned in Scripture. The cherubim were the guardians of the Garden of Eden.

> After he drove the man out, he placed on the east side of the Garden of Eden cherubim and a flaming

sword flashing back and forth to guard the way to the tree of life [Genesis 3:24].

Compare this with Webster's definition of *cherub*: "a beautiful usually winged child in painting and sculpture."

We do not know how long these cherubim were employed to guard the tree of life because it is not stated in Scripture. It is thought by some that this was a temporary measure, and the Garden was later removed. If not, perhaps these guardian cherubim remained on duty until the time the earth was destroyed by the flood. There is no record of cherubim appearing on the earth after the time of the Garden of Eden. Their likeness, however, was used frequently throughout the time of the tabernacle and the temple.

ARK OF THE COVENANT

God ordered Moses to place cherubim on the ark of the covenant, sometimes called the ark of the Testimony in the New International Version.

"And make two cherubim out of hammered gold at the ends of the cover" [Exodus 25:18].

No description or explanation of the cherubim seems to have been necessary, but some detail is given concerning the position and placing of the cherubim and their wings; "facing each other," and "wings spread upward."

Perhaps these people were familiar with the likeness of the cherubim through tradition and descriptions handed down by previous generations. The knowledge of the cherubim, however, could have been supplied by the Spirit of God in the same way the skill, ability and knowledge of crafts were supplied (Exodus 35:30-31).

The cherubim on the ark of the covenant would never have been seen by the people. They were not allowed to enter the Most Holy Place of the tabernacle where the ark was kept. When they traveled from one place to another and the ark was carried to the new location, it was completely covered.

When the camp is to move, Aaron and his sons are to go in and take down the shielding curtain and cover the ark of the Testimony with it [Numbers 4:5].

The space between the cherubim on the cover of the ark was the place where God's presence with the people was established, the place from which He spoke to them through Moses.

> When Moses entered the Tent of Meeting to speak with the Lord, he heard the voice speaking to him from between the two cherubim above the atonement cover on the ark of the Testimony. And he spoke with him [Numbers 7:89].

The atonement cover of the ark was viewed by Israel as the throne of their heavenly King. God's presence was found "between the cherubim." Throughout their wanderings, the Jews communicated with God through the manifestation of His presence between the cherubim of the ark of the covenant.

David's song of praise to God, after being delivered from Saul, was recorded in 2 Samuel 22 and Psalm 18. David pictured God being borne in flight on the wings of cherubim. "He mounted the cherubim and flew; he soared on the wings of the wind" [2 Samuel 22:11]. Psalm 18:10 repeats this verse, The wings of the cherubim symbolized the throne of God or the chariot of God. The chariot was said to be the cherubim in 1 Chronicles 28:18.

The cherubim were chosen by God as adornments for both the tabernacle and later the temple. The curtains for the tabernacle were embroidered with cherubim by skilled craftsmen. The curtain which separated the Holy Place from the Most Holy Place was also decorated with cherubim.

Solomon instructed the priests to place a pair of large cherubim statues in the Most Holy Place of the temple. The statues were placed on either side of the ark of the covenant. These golden statues were fifteen feet tall and their wings extended fifteen feet and filled the inner room of the temple. Surfaces inside the temple were also adorned with the likeness of the cherubim.

DESCRIPTION

In the many references to cherubim, no mention is made of their form, shape, or appearance until the Book of

Ezekiel. Ezekiel was a Jew, exiled in Babylon, when he was called to be a prophet of God. He was allowed to see visions which he described in great detail in chapter one as living creatures. Later, in chapter ten, Ezekiel revealed his recognition that the living creatures he had seen by the river were the cherubim.

These were the living creatures I had seen beneath the God of Israel by the Kebar River, and I realized that they were cherubim. Each had four faces and four wings, and under their wings was what looked like the hands of a man. Their faces had the same appearance as those I had seen by the Kebar River. . .[Ezekiel 10:20-22].

Ezekiel's description of the cherubim with four faces (cherub, man, lion, eagle), four wings, hands of a man, and entire bodies completely full of eyes, sounds grotesque when compared to the cupid-like cherub of our imagination. The function of cherubim as guardians of sacred or unapproachable objects is also in contrast to the sweet, sentimental, child-like cupid, often called a cherub.

The significance of the cherubim as guardians and the symbols of God's presence, is evidenced by the volume of biblical information concerning them. Although our study would be incomplete without a study of these beings, they are entirely different from the customary angel messengers who are our main focus.

Archaeological discoveries have revealed the remains of statues in the ruins of ancient civilizations, which the authorities say may have been representations of cherubim. These statues were composite creatures which were part man and part animal. Often they had a human face, an animal body, four legs, and a large pair of wings. They were similar to the winged statues of bulls or lions, with human heads, which were placed as guardians at the entrances of palaces and temples by pagan rulers.

The Assyrians built large representations of bulls with the head of a man and eagle's wings at the gateways of their palaces and temples to guard kings. In both Egyptian and Phoenician art, we find animal/human creatures with wings which shielded sacred places. The sphinxes of Egypt and Greece which guarded temples and tombs also bear some similarity to the cherubim.

Babylonians believed in supernatural creatures who guarded entrances to places of religious importance. Composite winged creatures were represented on the gates and entrances. They were also carved into the armrests of royal thrones as charms to protect against evil spirits. The cherubim of God preceded all these figures. Whatever God revealed of the cherubim was appropriated and modified by the pagan peoples of the world.

SERAPHIM

Another heavenly being which is not a class or kind of angel, is the seraph. The plural of the word *seraph is seraphim* or *seraphs*. The seraphim are not traditional angels, in fact, they are not angels at all. They are beings who exist in addition to angels. The word seraphim means "burning ones" and comes from a Hebrew root which means "burn." The same word is used to mean snakes in Numbers 21:6; Isaiah 14:29; and 30:6.

When Isaiah was called to be a prophet of God, he saw a vision of heaven. He described the seraphim as being above the Lord, who was seated on a throne. Isaiah does not give as much detail as Ezekiel did in describing the cherubim. The description of the seraphim only gives us the number and use of their wings.

> Above him were seraphs, each with six wings: With two wings they covered their faces, with two they covered their feet, and with two they were flying [Isaiah 6:2].

The activity of the seraphim is also recorded and information is included about their very powerful voices and what they said.

> And they were calling to one another: "Holy, holy, holy is the Lord Almighty; the whole earth is full of his glory." At the sound of their voices the doorposts and thresholds shook and the temple was filled with smoke [Isaiah 6:3-4].

Isaiah was afraid he would die because he had seen God. He expressed his feelings of guilt and impurity. Then a seraph touched his mouth with a coal from the altar and cleansed him for his work as a prophet.

Then one of the seraphs flew to me with a live coal in his hand, which he had taken with tongs from the altar. With it he touched my mouth and said, "See, this has touched your lips; your guilt is taken away and your sin atoned for" [Isaiah 6:6-7].

These references in the sixth chapter of Isaiah are the only mention of seraphim in the Old Testament. Although the seraphim are not specifically named in the New Testament, they are similar to the living creatures of John's vision.

. . .In the center, around the throne, were four living creatures, and they were covered with eyes, in front and in back. The first living creature was like a lion, the second was like an ox, the third had a face like a man, the fourth was like a flying eagle. Each of the four living creatures had six wings and was covered with eyes all around, even under his wings. Day and night they never stop saying: "Holy, holy, holy is the Lord God Almighty, who was, and is, and is to come" [Revelation 4:6-8].

The living creatures and the seraphim had these things in common: the number of wings, attendance at the throne, and continual praising of God. These living creatures also resemble those which Ezekiel identified as cherubim. The four living creatures and the cherubim were both covered with eyes. Instead of each living creature having four faces, as described by Ezekiel, here each one had a different face. Ezekiel described the faces of a cherub, a man, a lion, and an eagle. All four of the cherubim looked alike, but in Revelation, the living creatures were each different in appearance. One was like a lion, one an ox, a man, and an eagle. Notice the ox was substituted for the cherub of Ezekiel's description. Thus, the living creatures described by John are heavenly beings resembling the cherubim and seraphim, but they are not characteristic of the angel messengers of God.

SUMMARY

The only scriptural evidence that angels are ranked or classified is that one is called archangel. As a prefix "arch" means chief or principle. Thus, we know that Michael, the archangel, is elevated above the other angels. Although there are some references that present the concept of seven angels in an elevated position, only one archangel is mentioned in Scripture.

Michael and Gabriel are the only angels in the Bible to be called by proper names. In the Apocryphal books, two more names are given and in Jewish tradition many others are named.

The cherubim were favored as adornment for the ark of the covenant and tabernacle curtains. Their statues decorated the temple, and their likeness was carved on walls and furniture. Our only information concerning the seraphim is provided by Isaiah 6. The living creatures of Revelation are similar to the cherubim and seraphim.

The cherubim, seraphim, and living cretures described in the Bible are heavenly creatures who exist in addition to conventional angels. All these beings populate the heavenly realm. Angels, however, as this study defines them, are distinguished from the others as ministering spirits and messengers of God.

REVIEW

1. How many archangels are named in the Bible? Give names: _____

2. How many angels are named in the Bible? _____ Give names: _____

3. What is significant about Michael in addition to his role as archangel? _____

_____

4. What is significant about Gabriel?_____

_____

5. Do cherubim, seraphim and living creatures qualify as angels? If not, what are they?_____

_____

6. Describe a cherub. _____

7. How did God instruct Moses to use the likeness of cherubim? _____

8. Describe a seraph. _____

9. How do the living creatures of Revelation compare with the cherubim and seraphim? _____

NOTES

_____
_____
_____
_____
_____
_____
_____
_____
_____
_____
_____
_____
_____
_____
_____
_____
_____
_____
_____
_____
_____
_____

Chapter Five

Christ and The Angels

CHRIST SUPERIOR

Jesus Christ was in heaven with the angels before He came to earth as a man. He returned to the home of angels when He ascended from the earth back to heaven. Angels were a part of the events of His earthly life. By becoming a man and suffering death, He placed Himself "a little lower than the angels." When He returned to heaven, triumphant over death, all forces submitted to Him, including angels. When He descends again, He will come with His angels!

The writing which is commonly known as the Epistle of Paul to the Hebrews was recognized and accepted by the church in the second century. One of the reasons some attribute the authorship of this book to Paul, is that it was considered to have been Paul's writing at that time. When the canon of Scripture was accepted, the Book of Hebrews was regarded as the fourteenth epistle of Paul. The writer, however, does not identify himself, as Paul always did. Therefore, the Book of Hebrews is anonymous.

It is interesting to think about the consideration given to angels in the Book of Hebrews and in the epistles which can be identified with Paul. The word "angel" or "angels" appears fourteen times in the thirteen Epistles of Paul, which is not considered frequent usage. In the Book of Hebrews, however, the word "angels" is used twelve times in the first two chapters and a total of fourteen times in the entire book.

Although we do not know who the author was, he was known to those who received the letter — Jewish converts to Christianity. It must have been difficult for them to relinquish their ties with the strong influence of the Law of Moses. The writer may have feared that they would not remain faithful to Christ. He would also have been aware that in the centuries preceding the birth of Christ, the Jews had amplified the doctrine of angels. They had gradually magnified the purpose and power of angels from the time Judah fell under the influence of Babylon and Persia, during the Exile.

The theme of the Book of Hebrews is the complete superiority of Jesus Christ, the Son of God. The author wrote to Jewish converts to encourage them to continue in their Christianity. Chapters one and two compare the Son of God with the angels. We do not know whether the Hebrews worshiped angels as the Colossians did, but we do know they thought of angels as exalted beings.

Names were extremely important to people in biblical times. Do you remember a person in the Bible whose name was changed (Abraham, Sarah, Israel, Joshua, Peter, Paul)? Think of the occasions we considered in earlier chapters when an angel told someone what to name their unborn child (Ishmael, John, Jesus). The Jew of the Christian age also placed an unusual importance on the meaning of a person's name. We link a person's name with his reputation, but to them the name was synonymous with character.

Jesus is as much above the angels as His name is above the angels' names. The incomparable name given to Christ was "Son." Such an excellent name was never given to any angel.

> So he became as much superior to the angels as the name he has inherited is superior to theirs. For to which of the angels did God ever say, "You are my Son; today I have become your Father"? Or again, "I will be his Father, and he will be my Son"? [Hebrews 1:4-5].

As another comparison of Jesus with the angels, the writer told the Hebrews about Jesus in heaven sitting beside God. The right side symbolized the place of highest honor. Christ is reigning with God but angels are only servants of God.

> To which of the angels did God ever say, "Sit at my right hand until I make your enemies a footstool for your feet"? Are not all angels ministering spirits sent to serve those who will inherit salvation? [Hebrews 1:13-14].

This is only one of the references we find, in the Book of Hebrews, which says Christ is sitting on the right hand of God. Others passages are: Hebrews 1:3, 8:1, 10:12, 12:2.

The Ephesian letter also told us that Christ is seated at the right hand of God, and that He is superior to every being. In the first century, people concocted all kinds of supernatural creatures, in addition to angels and demons. Christ is above all these no matter what they were called.

> That power is like the working of his mighty strength, which he exerted in Christ when he raised him from the dead and seated him at his right hand in the heavenly realms, far above all rule and authority, power and dominion, and every title that can be given, not only in the present age but also in the one to come [Ephesians 1:19b-21].

Paul was not naming the ranks or levels of angels, but referring to divisions and classifications made by men. This is an indication that they expanded and exaggerated the teaching on angels during the time between the writing of the Old and New Testaments.

CHRIST'S MESSAGE SUPERIOR

The message spoken by angels was the law given to Moses on Mount Sinai. It is contrasted with the message of Christ, the gospel. If breaking the law given to Moses by angels was punished, defiance of Christ's law will receive a greater penalty. This gives further emphasis to the preeminence of Christ.

> For if the message spoken by angels was binding, and every violation and disobedience received its just punishment, how shall we escape if we ignore such a great salvation? [Hebrews 2:2-3a].

The people to whom this letter was written were Christians whose former religious practice was Judaism. We know the Jews gave angels a higher position than they should have and it is possible that their belief exalted angels to a position of ruling over them in eternity. The "world to come," will not be subject to angels.

> It is not to angels that he has subjected the world to come, about which we are speaking [Hebrews 2:5].

Another possible explanation for the statement is the author's fear that they were in danger of compromising Christ's teaching by combining it with Jewish law or even returning entirely to their former practice of Judaism.

Next the writer applies Psalms 8:4-6 to Christ to illustrate His excellence over the angels. Though He became lower than the angels for a time, He is now restored to His place of supremacy. Continuing to draw from the eighth Psalm, the writer says that man was made slightly inferior to the angels.

> But there is a place where someone has testified: What is man that you are mindful of him, the son of man that you care for him?"
> You made him a little lower than the angels; you crowned him with glory and honor [Hebrews 2:6-7].

Still applying Psalm 8 to Jesus, the writer says He was made "a little lower than the angels" when He became a man in order to die for us.

> But we see Jesus, who was made a little lower than the angels, now crowned with glory and honor because he suffered death, so that by the grace of God he might taste death for everyone [Hebrews 2:9].

He became superior to angels again when He was victorious over death and the grave.

When we consider our salvation we see that even man is superior to angels in one respect. Apparently the angels do not have an opportunity to repent of wrong. When angels sinned, they were put out of heaven. Christ came to redeem man, He does not save the sinful angels.

For surely it is not angels he helps, but Abraham's descendants [Hebrews 2:16].

ANGELS WORSHIP CHRIST

The Book of Hebrews repeatedly contrasted the superiority of Jesus Christ with the angels. Since the angels were highly revered by the Christians who were converts from Judaism, this was a significant comparison. To impress upon them the elevated position of Jesus, the writer of Hebrews emphasizes that even the angels, whom they exalted, worshiped Jesus.

And again, when God brings his firstborn into the world, he says, "Let all God's angels worship him" [Hebrews 1:6].

MAN WORSHIPED ANGELS

The writer of the Book of Hebrews contrasted and compared Christ to the prophets, the priests, and the angels. He proved Christ to be superior to all of them. We do not know the extent of the error concerning angels by the Hebrew Christians, but we can see that a problem existed which made it necessary to teach these lessons. The Jews had increased reverence for angels because of angelic involvement in giving the law to Moses. We know that this exaltation of angels was wrong. We do not know whether this error had grown to the extent that angels were objects of worship by the Hebrew Christians.

There is more evidence in the case of the Colossians of angel worship. Although Paul does not go into detail about the false teaching which existed at Colosse, some think there were seeds of Gnostic teaching already present. In the second century, the Gnostics taught that God could only be approached through the medium of angelic beings. Paul must have seen the beginnings of this doctrine at the time he wrote the Colossian letter (c. 60 A.D.).

The people had assigned rank and classification to the angels. Thus, Paul used their own terms to teach that Christ is superior to all.

For by him all things were created: things in heaven and on earth, visible and invisible, whether thrones or powers or rulers or authorities; all things were created by him and for him [Colossians 1:16].

Paul's use of these terms: thrones, powers, rulers, authorities, indicates that the teaching of a hierarchy of angels was a part of the problem of the Colossians.

Notice Paul's warning. It is apparent that the false doctrine of worshiping angels was also being taught at Colosse.

Do not let anyone who delights in false humility and the worship of angels disqualify you for the prize. Such a person goes into great detail about what he has seen, and his unspiritual mind puffs him up with idle notions [Colossians 2:18].

In addition to the Colossian error, angel worship also existed among the Essenes, a secluded Jewish sect. We think that the manuscripts called "The Dead Sea Scrolls" were the work of the Essene sect. Josephus tells us that they claimed to be the guardians of "the names of the angels." He says that a convert to this sect was required to swear many oaths. One of these was to preserve "the names of the angels."

The Scripture teaches that God is a jealous God, and that He prohibited the Israelites from bowing down to idols (Exodus 20:5). We know that He alone is to be worshiped.

Fear the Lord your God, serve him only and take your oaths in his name [Deuteronomy 6:13].

When Jesus was being tempted by the devil He responded by quoting Scripture. Each time He answered with a passage from the Book of Deuteronomy. Satan offered to give Him "all the kingdoms of the world," if Jesus would worship him.

Jesus said to him, "Away from me Satan! For it is written: 'Worship the Lord your God and serve him only'" [Matthew 4:10].

The worshiping of angels is specifically forbidden by Scripture. Two examples are given of John attempting to worship an angel. Each time the angel stopped John just as Peter stopped Cornelius from worshiping him (Acts 10:25-26).

Then the angel said to me, "Write: 'Blessed are those who are invited to the wedding supper of the Lamb!' " And he added, "These are the true words of God."

At this I fell at his feet to worship him. But he said to me, "Do not do it!" I am a fellow servant with you and with your brothers who hold to the testimony of Jesus. Worship God! For the testimony of Jesus is the spirit of prophecy" [Revelation 19:9-10].

I, John, am the one who heard and saw these things. And when I had heard and seen them, I fell down to worship at the feet of the angel who had been showing them to me. But he said to me, "Do not do it!" I am a fellow servant with you and with your brothers the prophets and of all who keep the words of this book. Worship God!" [Revelation 22:8-9].

ANGELS AND CHRIST'S BIRTH

Throughout the record of the birth of Christ, there are repeated references to the participation of angels. The angel Gabriel told Mary that she would be the mother of the Savior. An angel explained Mary's pregnancy to Joseph, to whom she was promised. Jesus' birth announcement was made by an angel to a group of shepherds. This angel was joined by a large group of other angels who praised God and said,

"Glory to God in the highest, and on earth peace to men on whom his favor rests" [Luke 2:14].

It was an angel who warned Joseph in a dream to take Jesus and Mary and escape to Egypt. Later, Joseph was informed by an angel, in a dream, when it was safe for them to return.

CHRIST'S TEACHING ON ANGELS

In His ministry on earth, Jesus often taught concerning the angels of heaven. He said that angels guarded His followers who became humble, as little children. Although Jesus had spoken of children earlier in the chapter, these "little ones" are His disciples. The reference changes from "a little child" in verse two, to one who becomes "like this child" in verse four. We learn from verse six that He is speaking of "little ones who believe" in Him.

> But if anyone causes one of these little ones who believe in me to sin, it would be better for him to have a large millstone hung around his neck and to be drowned in the depths of the sea [Matthew 18:6].

These angels were watching over the disciples and they had unlimited access to God's presence. Some have enlarged and extended this to mean that every person, particularly every little child, has a guardian angel who has continuous admittance to the presence of God.

> See that you do not look down on one of these little ones. For I tell you that their angels in heaven always see the face of my Father in heaven [Matthew 18:10].

Jesus wanted His disciples to be His advocates. He taught them that if they were ashamed of Him, He will also be ashamed of them when He returns with the angels.

> If anyone is ashamed of me and my words in this adulterous and sinful generation; the Son of Man will be ashamed of him when he comes in his Father's glory with the holy angels [Mark 8:38].

> If anyone is ashamed of me and my words, the Son of Man will be ashamed of him when he comes, in his glory and in the glory of the Father and of the holy angels [Luke 9:26].

He later said to the disciples, before a large crowd, that declaring or denying Him before men would determine whether He disowns them in the presence of the angels of God.

> I tell you, whoever acknowledges me before men, the Son of Man will also acknowledge him before the

angels of God. But he who disowns me before men will be disowned before the angels of God [Luke 12:8-9].

In the Book of Revelation, John also records Christ's teaching concerning those He will acknowledge before the angels.

He who overcomes will, like them, be dressed in white. I will never blot out his name from the book of life, but will acknowledge his name before my Father and his angels [Revelation 3:5].

The Pharisees criticized Jesus, complaining that He associated with sinners, and even ate with them. Jesus taught them with parables of a lost sheep and a lost coin. He said that rejoicing occurs in heaven when one sinner repents. The rejoicing He spoke of is taking place in the presence of the angels. Although this may include the angels, Jesus did not say that the angels rejoice.

I tell you that in the same way there will be more rejoicing in heaven over one sinner who repents than over ninety-nine righteous persons who do not need to repent [Luke 15:7].

In the same way, I tell you, there is rejoicing in the presence of the angels of God over one sinner who repents [Luke 15:10].

The Sadducees did not accept the expanded teaching of the Pharisees on angels. In fact, they entirely rejected belief in angels and resurrection from death. They accepted only the first five books of the Old Testament, as authoritative. Once they attempted to trap Jesus with a trick question about which of her seven husbands would be the mate of a particular woman at the resurrection. Jesus began His reply by condemning their lack of knowledge of the Scriptures. He told them that the resurrected saints will not marry but will, in this respect, be like the angels who do not have marriage relationships.

At the resurrection, people will neither marry nor be given in marriage; they will be like the angels in heaven [Matthew 22:30].

ANGELS MINISTER TO CHRIST

Twice in the earthly life of Jesus, it is recorded that He received the ministry of angels. We do not know what the nature of their ministry to Him was. He had been fasting, in the desert for forty days, and we know from Scripture that "he was hungry" (Matthew 4:2; Luke 4:2). Therefore, some suppose that the angels brought food to Jesus. There is, however, no evidence that the angels fed Jesus.

He had also suffered the temptation of the devil. Satan used his best efforts to test Jesus. Each time Jesus overcame temptation by quoting Scripture to Satan. After being in the desert for forty days and being tempted by Satan, His needs must have been much greater than just physical hunger.

Then the devil left him, and angels came and attended him [Matthew 4:11].

The definition of the word, *diakoneo* in the original Greek, which is here translated "attended," has the meaning "to be a servant, attendant, to serve, wait upon, minister" (Vine *Expository Dictionary of New Testament Words*, III:348).

...and he was in the desert forty days, being tempted by Satan. He was with the wild animals, and the angels attended him [Mark 1:13].

Luke does not record this occasion of the angels attending Christ, but he is the only Gospel writer to record the ministry of an angel who strengthened Jesus as He prayed on the Mount of Olives before He was arrested.

And angel from heaven appeared to him and strengthened him [Luke 22:43].

ANGELS AND THE RESURRECTION OF CHRIST

After His Crucifixion, Jesus' body was requested by Joseph, a wealthy man from the town of Arimathea in Judah. Joseph was a member of the Sanhedrin, but did not concur with the Council's verdict in Jesus' case. Luke described him as a good man who waited for God's kingdom (Luke 23:50-51). Joseph, assisted by Nicodemus (John 19:39), prepared the body of Jesus for burial. Matthew and Mark told us that a stone was placed at the entrance of the tomb where Jesus' body was placed.

The chief priests and the Pharisees remembered that Jesus told them He would rise again after three days. Fearing that the disciples would try to steal the body and claim that He arose from death, they asked for a guard at the tomb. Pilate ordered the tomb guarded by Roman soldiers.

> So they went and made the tomb secure by putting a seal on the stone and posting the guard [Matthew 27:66].

On the morning following the Sabbath the women, knowing nothing of the guard at the tomb, came to visit the grave. Mark records their concern about removing the heavy stone which closed the tomb.

> Very, early on the first day of the week, just after sunrise, they were on their way to the tomb and they asked each other, "Who will roll the stone away from the entrance of the tomb?" [Mark 16:2-3].

When they arrived at the burial place this task, which would have been difficult for the women, was already done by an angel.

> There was a violent earthquake, for an angel of the Lord came down from heaven and, going to the tomb, rolled back the stone and sat on it [Matthew 28:2].

The record of the Gospels show different aspects of the same occurrence. Mark described the appearance of a young man, at the tomb, whom Matthew identified as an angel. Luke and John said there were two of them. Luke calls them men, however, we know from John's record that they were angels. Matthew and Mark may have mentioned only the angel who spoke to the women.

> His appearance was like lightning, and his clothes were white as snow [Matthew 28:3].

As they entered the tomb, they saw a young man dressed in a white robe sitting on the right side, and they were alarmed [Mark 16:5].

While they were wondering about this, suddenly two men in clothes that gleamed like lightning stood beside them [Luke 24:4].

Then the disciples went back to their homes, but Mary stood outside the tomb crying. As she wept, she bent over to look into the tomb and saw two angels in white, seated where Jesus' body had been, one at the head and the other at the foot [John 20:10-12].

The angels reassured the frightened women that they would find Jesus in Galilee, and reminded them that He had foretold His death and resurrection (Luke 24:5-7).

ANGELS AND THE ASCENSION OF CHRIST

Forty days after the resurrection of Jesus, while He was blessing His disciples, He left them and returned to heaven. We believe that the two men who spoke to the disciples were angels.

They were looking intently up into the sky as he was going, when suddenly two men dressed in white stood beside them.

"Men of Galilee," they said, "why do you stand here looking into the sky? This same Jesus, who has been taken from you into heaven, will come back in the same way you have seen him go into heaven" [Acts 1:10-11].

Jesus existed in heaven with God and the angels before He became a man. He taught His disciples that He would return to heaven.

What if you see the Son of Man ascend to where he was before! [John 6:62].

Jesus Christ, having returned to heaven, now reigns at God's right hand. Every possible order of beings, both good and evil, is now yielding to and obeying Him.

It saves you by the resurrection of Jesus Christ, who has gone into heaven and is at God's right hand —with angels, authorities and powers in submission to him [1 Peter 3:21b-22].

Paul wrote to Timothy concerning "the mystery of godliness." One of the things he specifically mentions about Jesus is that He was "seen of angels." Angels observed the life of Jesus as He resided here on earth. It was a unique experience for them to witness His manifestation in a mortal body.

Beyond all question, the mystery of godliness is great: He appeared in a body, was vindicated by the Spirit, was seen by angels, as preached among the nations, was believed on in the world, was taken up in glory [1 Timothy 3:16].

Angels were a part of the earthly life of Christ. They notified His parents and proclaimed His birth. Angels served Him when He was in deep distress. They announced His resurrection and explained His ascension. Angels will accompany Him when He descends again.

THE ANGEL OF THE REVELATION

John received his revelation from an angel sent by Jesus. This particular angel was identified by possessive pronouns in the Book of Revelation. John said he was "his angel," that is Jesus' angel; and Jesus called him "my angel."

The revelation of Jesus Christ, which God gave him to show his servants what must soon take place. He made it known by sending his angel to his servant John [Revelation 1:1].

I, Jesus, have sent my angel to give you this testimony for the churches. I am the Root and the Offspring of David, and the bright Morning Star [Revelation 22:16].

Since these pronouns were only used elsewhere with reference to God's angel, the angel of the Lord, this indicates a special angel who was sent by Jesus to bring His revelation to John.

ANGELS AND THE RETURN OF CHRIST

Jesus predicted His death and told the disciples of the time when He would come again. He described this as a time that angels would accompany and assist Him. He taught His disciples that when He comes to earth again, He will come with His angels. We notice again the possessive pronoun which now refers to a group of angels.

For the Son of Man is going to come in his Father's glory with his angels, and then he will reward each person according to what he has done [Matthew 16:27].

When Jesus returns the angels will accompany Him and He will sit in final judgment of all nations.

When the Son of Man comes in his glory, and all the angels with him, he will sit on his throne in heavenly glory [Matthew 25:31].

The following verse refers to "powerful angels." Some people say this is a class of angels given special power to do God's will. It is more likely an allusion to the strength of all God's angels.

God is just: He will pay back trouble to those who trouble you and give relief to you who are troubled, and to us as well. This will happen when the Lord Jesus is revealed from heaven in blazing fire with his powerful angels [2 Thessalonians 1:6-7].

These angels will gather the righteous with the sound of the trumpet. The sounding of the trumpet was an important signal in Jewish tradition. The trumpet sounded on the first day of every month and they were commanded to mark the beginning of the seventh month (Jewish New Year) with "trumpet blasts" (Leviticus 23:24).

And he will send his angels with a loud trumpet call, and they will gather his elect from the four winds, from one end of the heavens to the other [Matthew 24:31].

And he will send his angels and gather his elect from the four winds, from the ends of the earth to the ends of the heavens [Mark 13:27].

SUMMARY

The writer of the Book of Hebrews effectively illustrates that Jesus Christ is superior to the angels. Christ was subordinate to angels only when he became human. Jesus' preeminence is demonstrated by the angels themselves, who worshiped Him.

Because an exaggeration of the role and function of angels entered into Jewish belief, unscriptural acts were practiced. These angels who are inferior to Christ, once were actually, erroneously worshiped by man.

At every stage of the earthly life of Christ, He was "seen by angels." They foretold His birth to Mary and Joseph, and announced the great event to shepherds. Many of the teachings that Jesus gave His disciples involved the angels. They ministered to Him twice at low points in His earthly life. The angels attended Christ's resurrection from death and witnessed His ascension to heaven. He is reigning today in heaven, at God's right hand, where angels are subordinate to Him. They will be with Him when He comes again.

REVIEW

1. What is the theme of the Book of Hebrews?

   _____

2. What is meant by the "message spoken by angels?"

   _____

3. What false doctrine was taught at Colosse? _____

   _____

4. Who attempted to worship an angel but was forbidden? _____

5. List the ways angels took part in the life of Jesus from prenatal through infancy. _____

   _____

6. List three or more teachings of Christ concerning angels. _____

_____

_____

7. What two times did Jesus receive the ministry of angels? _____

_____

8. What part will angels play in the return of Christ?

_____

_____

NOTES

_____

_____

_____

_____

_____

_____

_____

_____

_____

_____

_____

_____

_____

_____

_____

_____

_____

_____

_____

_____

_____

_____

Chapter Six

Influence Of The Jews

We have now surveyed the fundamental Scriptures which pertain to angels. We learned that the angel who comes from the pages of the Bible is very far removed from that "treetop angel" we discussed earlier. Therefore, we shall begin to explore the things which may have directed us to an altered perception of God's angels.

SIGNFICANCE OF JEWISH HISTORY

One event which is responsible for changes in the understanding of angels is the direction of Jewish history. The Jews were made subservient by other nations for hundreds of years. When they came in contact with different languages, it changed their speech. When they were touched by various customs, their habits changed. When they were exposed to other religions, one result was a change in their concept of the spirit world, including angels. The oppression of the Jews was to continue so that they experienced the culture and tradition of a society dominated by Near Eastern influence for thousands of years. The events of this time are responsible for shaping the world in which the Christian era began.

EXILE IN BABYLON

The Babylonian Exile was responsible, in part, for the changes that occurred in the way angels were perceived in ancient times. In 931 B.C., under the leadership of

Jeroboam, ten of the Hebrew tribes rebelled and the kingdom was divided. These ten tribes formed the northern kingdom, Israel, which existed until 722 B.C., when the majority were deported by the Assyrians, and lost to history.

The other two tribes, the kingdom of Judah, existed as a small nation until the armies of Babylonia conquered and drove them into exile in 605 B.C. More Jews were exiled in 597 and 587 B.C. In Babylon, they were treated quite well and began to assimilate Babylonian culture. They adopted the Babylonian calendar and learned to speak the Aramaic language.

This change in the language was one result of the Exile in Babylon. Apparently they learned to speak Aramaic to communicate with their captors. The Aramaic language was very well received by the Jews. Their speech became mixed with Aramaic until finally, some spoke Aramaic entirely. It was customary to read from the Hebrew Scripture in the synagogue. For those who did not speak Hebrew, an interpretation was required to understand the reading of Scripture. It became popular to follow the reading of the Hebrew with an oral paraphrase so the Aramaic-speaking Jew might understand. This is a possible explanation of Nehemiah 8:8.

> They read from the Book of the Law of God, making it clear and giving the meaning so that the people could understand what was being read.

These paraphrase interpretations were called *Targums*, and were expanded into lectures, making application of the reading. Some time later, these talks were put into writing. Originally, they were simple explanations of the text but the paraphrasing became quite liberal.

INFLUENCE OF EXILE

The Exile was most influential in shaping the future lives of the Jewish people, and it was responsible for extreme changes in their form of worship. The Jews could only offer sacrifices to God at the Jerusalem Temple. Now they were separated from the Temple which had been the center of their religious life. God's law did not allow them to construct a Temple in Babylon. Judaism was forced to abandon sacrificial offerings and begin to focus on a personal relationship with God. Their solution was to concentrate on what was available to them. They turned to study and interpretation of the Torah (Jewish Scripture and other sacred literature). Scripture reading and prayer were intensified because they were not limited to a particular location.

When the Jews returned to Jerusalem, they rebuilt the Temple, and resumed worship through sacrifice.

> Then Jeshua, son of Jozadak and his fellow priests and Zerubbabel, son of Shealtiel and his associates, began to build the altar of the God of Israel to sacrifice burnt offerings on it, in accordance with what is written in the Law of Moses, the man of God. Despite their fear of the peoples around them, they built the altar on its foundation and sacrificed burnt offerings on it to the Lord, both the morning and evening sacrifices [Ezra 3:2-3].

GROWTH OF SYNAGOGUES

Although they resumed worship in the traditional manner, the synagogue became the center of religious life. Jewish tradition says that the synagogue developed during the Exile in Babylon. While separated from the ceremonial Temple worship, the people needed to have a place of fellowship, study and prayer. Synagogues developed gradually but retained popularity even after the return from exile and reconstruction of the Temple. By the time of Jesus' ministry, synagogues were located in every community where there were ten adult male Jews. In addition to the ritual Temple worship, the synagogues were also places of worship.

In addition to the change in their concept of angels, the Jews also brought back Babylonian knowledge of astronomy and the Babylonian way of counting time. The planets were named for their Babylonian gods and we continue to identify them through the Greco-Roman form of these names. In Babylonian belief, the days of the week were ruled by these planets. They devoted each day of the week to one of their deities. The names by which we call days of the week come from the Roman form of these names.

PERSIAN PERIOD/450 - 330 B.C.

In 538 B.C., Cyrus king of Persia, conquered Babylon, and the Jewish captives were ruled by the Persians. The Jews were treated well under this rule. Cyrus allowed self-respect among conquered people and he soon permitted some of them to return to Judah under Zerubbabel. Others, however, did not wish to return; having integrated themselves into Babylonian life. Those who returned to Judah built an altar and began to offer daily sacrifices which were interrupted in 587 B.C.

The second group, under Ezra's direction, returned to Judah in 458 B.C., and the final group led by Nehemiah, in 432 B.C. For about 200 years after this, the Persians controlled Judah without interference in their religious observances. At the time of the close of the Old Testament, about 400 B.C., there was still no independent Hebrew kingdom. Even the people who had returned to Judah were still the subjects of Persia and would remain so until the conquest by Alexander the Great of Greece.

Under Persian control and exposure to their myth and religion, the Jews developed a fascination for angels, and demons. They took the Persian view of the universe with its complex spirit world. This resulted in a marked growth in angelology. Hierarchies of angels were introduced in Jewish thought as a result of exposure to these beliefs.

HELLENISTIC PERIOD/330 - 166 B.C.

Alexander the Great conquered the Near East (334-332 B.C.) bringing the Jews under Grecian rule which had a lasting effect on Judaism. Alexander believed he could unite the world through the power of Greek culture. He was a benevolent ruler to the Jews, allowing observance of their religious laws and permitting them to enjoy the advantages of the Greeks.

As a result of this victory, the Jews adopted the Greek language which prepared the way for the translation of the Old Testament into Greek, by Ptolemy II. This translation, the Septuagint, was the foundation for Jewish classics in the Greek language. In Alexandria and throughout Egypt, the non-Jewish world became acquainted with the Holy Scriptures through the Septuagint.

At the same time Jews, even in Palestine, began to adopt the behavior of Hellenistic culture. The Hellenistic age marked the merging of Jewish teaching with Greek culture, especially from 300 to 200 B.C. This was responsible for the spread of many new ideas which made an impression on the Jews. They borrowed concepts of Greek origin, and previously unknown beliefs were incorporated into their theology.

The Jews became alienated from God and did not maintain the close personal relationship they had in the past. They exalted Him beyond the possibility of personal contact, refusing to utter His name. These acts of reverence created the need for mediators between man and God. As this elevation of God occurred, the emphasis on angels as intermediaries increased.

When Alexander the Great died in 323 B.C., his domain was divided among his generals because they lacked the strength to succeed him. Two of these divisions were of distinct interest to the Jews—the Ptolemies and the Selucids. They were treated kindly during the reign of Ptolemy II and he authorized the translation of their sacred writings, the Pentateuch, (first five books of Old Testament) into Greek, the original Septuagint. In the Selucid Empire, however, Judah was gravely persecuted by Antiochus II.

MACCABEAN PERIOD /167 - 63 B.C.

Antiochus II, (175-164 B.C.) the Selucid ruler, was determined to force Greek culture on the Jews. The laws were carried out with excessive cruelty; Judaism was forbidden, and the Temple profaned. Led by an old priest, Mattathias, and his five sons, the Jews revolted against this treatment. By about 165 B.C., Judas Maccabaeus, one of the sons of Mattathias, was able to cleanse and rededicate the Temple and restore the religious life of the Jews. In 142 B.C., twenty-five years after the revolt began, Maccabaeus' brother, Simon, secured the independence of the Jews and Jerusalem was free from foreign rule for the first time in 445 years. This independence would last only about eighty years.

The two apocryphal books, 1 and 2 Maccabees, describe the events of the Maccabean Revolt. They were written independently by two historians; 1 Maccabees about 100 B.C., and 2 Maccabees after 124 B.C. These books were not included in the Hebrew canon of Scripture.

SADDUCEES

One result of the Selucid persecution and Maccabean resistance was the development of Jewish sects, the Sadducees, and the Pharisees. The Sadducees were opposed to the revolt of the Maccabees, preferring Greek culture to the body of law developed by the scribes. The Sadducees accepted only the first five books of the Old Testament—the Pentateuch. The Oral Law, which had grown out of the interpretation of the Scripture as it applied to daily living, did not obligate the Sadducees.

Since the doctrine of immortality and resurrection does not appear in the first five books of Scripture, the Sadducees rejected this belief. They also excluded the exaggerated, post-exilic, doctrine of angels, for the same reason. This denial was so characteristic of the difference in beliefs of the Sadducees and the Pharisees that Luke wrote,

> The Sadducees say that there is no resurrection, and that there are neither angels nor spirits, but the Pharisees acknowledge them all [Acts 23:8].

PHARISEES

The Pharisees were a group which allowed no compromise with the Greek way of life. They were subject to both the written and oral forms of the Law. They were responsible for the oral law being expanded and handed down through the years. The oral law later became the Mishna and the Talmud. Although the Pharisees were stricter, the Sadducees were more conservative. The Pharisees were hypocritical but very conscientious in observing the law.

92

The Pharisees were advocates of human equality, and emphasized ethical rather than theological teaching. They accepted the material contained in the oral tradition as equal with Scripture in inspiration and authority. Belief in future life, immortality of the soul, and reward and punishment after death, were taught by the Pharisees. They developed and accepted a hierarchy of angels and demons.

ROMAN PERIOD /63 B.C. - THROUGH NEW TESTAMENT PERIOD

Pompey, the Roman General, captured Jerusalem in 63 B.C., a little over a hundred years from the beginning of the Maccabean rebellion, and Palestine experienced still another power—Rome. Julius Caesar appointed Herod governor of Galilee in 47 B.C. Herod promised to enlarge and rebuild the Temple. Later he became king and was the ruler at the time of the birth of Jesus. Soon after the death of Jesus, the people began to oppose the Roman Empire but it would remain in power for centuries and every possible means would be used in efforts to annihilate Christianity.

JEWISH LITERATURE

SEPTUAGINT VERSION

Our Scriptural heritage pertaining to angels was greatly corrupted by ancient Jewish literature. This began with the translation of Hebrew Scriptures into the Greek language, the Septuagint. As a result of the cultural developments under Alexander, the first five books of the Old Testament were translated into the Greek language. Ptolemy II provided this translation for the Jews about 285 B.C. The Septuagint translation made the Scriptures available not only to the Greek-speaking Jew, but the entire Greek-speaking world as well. Later, other books of Scripture and some noncanonical books were included in the Septuagint Version and were widely used during the Christian era.

The fourteen apocryphal books were never allowed in the Hebrew Bible, but were included in the Septuagint Version. This was the Bible of the Jews outside Palestine, who no longer spoke Hebrew. It was also the Bible which the early Christians used. When New Testament writers quoted from the Old Testament Scriptures, they often quoted from the Septuagint Version. The Greek-speaking Jew of Alexandria in Egypt used the Septuagint version, including apocryphal books, as the Word of God. Thus, the apocryphal books were read by the early church as Scripture. Inclusion in the Septuagint version gave the apocryphal writings wide circulation. It would be difficult to overestimate the amount of influence the Septuagint version had on the Jews.

JEWISH APOCRYPHA

During the time between the Old and New Testaments, Jewish literature developed known as the Apocrypha and the Pseudepigrapha. The Apocrypha are writings omitted from the Hebrew canon, but included in the Greek Septuagint version. The word *apocrypha* is from a Greek word which means "secret" or "hidden." At one time the word described all the books which were excluded from the canon of Scripture. However, the term now refers to the Jewish books which were included in the Septuagint version but not in the Hebrew canon.

The Roman Catholic Church and the Eastern Orthodox Church officially accepted the Apocrypha at the Council of Trent in 1546 A.D. At this time the apocryphal books were dropped from the Protestant Bible. Before the Reformation in the sixteenth century A.D., however, they were commonly used by most Christians. The widespread use of the Septuagint may be responsible for the preservation of the books by the Catholic Church today.

These books and additions to canonical books of the Old Testament are as follows:

I Maccabees	Sirach	Susanna
II Maccabees	Wisdom	Bel and the Dragon
Tobit	Baruch	Addition to Esther
Judith	Prayer of Azariah	

The list originally included three more books which some Episcopalian and Lutheran collections include today. They are:

1 Esdras

2 Esdras   The Prayer of Manasseh

Some consider the apocryphal books as religious fiction, others a valuable reference source to the Intertestamental Period of history. Since the Old Testament canon closed about 400 B.C., these books are often considered necessary for historical information.

When the Bible was first printed in the English language, the Apocrypha were included as a matter of course. Later, there was a steadily increasing tendency to omit these books. In 1535, the Coverdale Bible was the first to separate the apocryphal books. Coverdale placed them at the close of the Old Testament with an introduction explaining they were less authoritative. It was not until 1599 that English Bibles excluded the Apocrypha. The apocryphal books supplied the readers with information about angels which is not found in the Scripture.

JEWISH PSEUDEPIGRAPHA

The Pseudepigrapha are writings not permitted in any collection of the Scriptures and falsely attributed to influential biblical characters. In Greek the word *pseudepigrapha* means "things falsely ascribed." Thus the term refers to a group of Jewish religious works, written under fictitious names, in the period 200 B.C. to 200 A.D. Some of these works have only become available to us in the last two centuries, but they were favorite reading of the early Christians.

It is entirely foreign to the nature of a writer to release his work without recognition; or what is even less likely, to give credit to someone else. There are several reasons why the pseudepigraphal books were ascribed to false authors. First, by attaching the name of a respected peson who had lived in an earlier time, the writer hoped to give credence to the work.

Another justification was that in this manner the author attempted to predate the time of his writing. Thus, the writer could take an event that had already occurred, write a "prophecy" of the event, and cause readers to believe it was prophesied beforehand. At times Christians did this in a sincere attempt to impress their religious belief on their heathen neighbors. The danger of persecution was another reason for the author to remain anonymous. By giving the name of an earlier writer to his own work, he placed it into circulation without the risk of punishment.

In the psuedepigraphal books great detail is given concerning the angels and the heavens. This is information which is not available in the accepted Scripture. It is in sharp contrast to Paul's statement in 2 Corithians 12:4 about being taken up to the third heaven. "He heard inexpressible things, things that man is not permitted to tell."

Even though these books were never given canonical status, some were read publicly to the churches for edification. The Book of Enoch, for instance, was highly regarded in New Testament times. In fact, Jude 14 and 15 is a quotation from this book.

Books were produced entirely by hand, and so they were quite rare. Inasmuch as they were used publicly, and availability was limited, pseudepigraphal works were sometimes produced in codex form in the same volume with books of Scripture. They were sometimes read to the assembled church.

DEAD SEA SCROLLS

In 1947, at Qumran, in a cave near the Dead Sea, an Arab boy made one of the world's greatest biblical, archaeological discoveries. The cave contained scrolls and fragments of documents dating back to the time of Christ. A great deal has been said about the importance of this discovery to Christianity. Some of the biblical matter which this find made accessible is at least a thousand years older, therefore closer to the original, than the texts previously available. It reflects the accuracy with which these manuscripts had been duplicated and it contributes to our understanding of the ancient language.

It is also highly significant that the majority of the manuscripts called "The Dead Sea Scrolls" are not of books that are now included in the canon of Scripture. They contain works attributed to the Essene sect, as well as apocryphal, pseudepigraphal, and apocalyptic writings. Out of a total of about 600 manuscripts, nearly 500 pertain to the nonbiblical categories mentioned. This is especially meaningful for research of the history of New Testament times. These books, which represent angels in a way quite foreign to their portrayal in Scripture, were readily available to the early church.

ESSENES

The documents found at Qumran are thought to be the remains of the work of a group of Essenes, a Jewish religious sect, who may have lived in this area from about 100 B.C. to about 70 A.D. They were a small group who withdrew themselves to maintain their purity. The Essenes lived in a sequestered type society and they practiced strict self-denial. They were preparing for a final war between the "Sons of Light" and "the Sons of Darkness."

The sect based their religious beliefs on the doctrine of the Two Spirits. They believed that the forces of good and evil were represented by Light and Darkness. The evil influence was called the "Angel of Darkness." It was his mission to lead astray those who were virtuous.

JEWISH LEGEND

An abundance of Jewish fable and legend has existed for thousands of years. Legend or fable is an essential means of imparting the Jewish message. These stories teach morality, and are traditionally told to young children. Thus, the Jew may be more familiar with Bible characters from legend than from Scripture. From the very earliest times, Jews borrowed from their pagan neighbors and adapted the stories to fit their own monotheistic religious outlook. This was done by placing the angels in roles of lesser gods of their polytheistic acquaintances. As a result of the influence of the Persians, during their Exile in Babylon, the Jews created hierarchies of angels. At this time, Jewish legend added three archangels: Gabriel, Raphael, and Uriel, to Michael, the only archangel disclosed in Scripture.

JEWISH MYSTICISM

The Jewish mysticism, or *Kabbalah* brought about profound transformations in the concept of the world, God, and other things in Judaism. The writing usually begins with a verse of Scripture, much as any other Bible commentary. Here the similarity ends. The mystic's information for this commentary was gained from meditation, reflection, and speculation. A favorite subject of the mystics was the angels and their intermediary functions between God and man. Because of continuing theoretical changes, impressions from outside the Bible entered into the teachings of mysticism.

There is a legend which says that the Kabbalah was brought down from heaven by the angels. This was allegedly after the fall of Adam for the purpose of restoring him to harmony with God. Contemplation on the heavens, angels, and demons were quite popular subjects among Jewish mystics from 200 B.C. to 100 A.D.

Mystics gave supernatural beings, such as angels, a very high position in their hierarchy of characters. An example of such a character is Metatron, who is identified as the angel Enoch became after he ascended into heaven. Mysticism continued to develop in various forms and had great appeal for first century Christians.

JEWISH AUTHORITATIVE WRITINGS

In addition to the Septuagint, the Apocrypha, the Pseudepigrapha, and the Dead Sea Scrolls, the Jews produced other literature. The *Talmud* is the authoritative body of Jewish law and teaching. It is considered to be the Code of Law of the Jews. It was written from the oral laws which resulted from the application of Scripture to everyday life. The *Mishna* was written by the Jews and completed about 200 A.D. It is a collection of Jewish traditions and became a part of the Talmud.

SUMMARY

The effect brought about by the course of history had a direct relation to the changes in Jewish beliefs concerning angels. When these people were taken from their own land and forced to live in exile among pagan races, the assimilation of knowledge relating to spirit beliefs altered their impressions of God's angels.

The Jews, after return to Judah, continued to be subservient to their conquerors. The Persian religion exerted influence on Jewish people regarding the spirit world. These modifications were tolerated and later accepted by faithful Jews.

The Jews were further persuaded to accept false information by the gradual changes that took place in their religious beliefs and practices. As the quantity of oral law increased, more credence was given to the magnified doctrines of angelology.

The acceptance of Greek culture caused the Jews to incorporate further changes into their religious practices. They elevated God beyond personal relationship. They believed it was necesssary to have an intermediary angel to communicate for them.

The Jewish sects, the Sadducees and the Pharisees, illustrate the extremes of belief relating to the angels. The Sadducees rejected belief in angels entirely. At the same time the Pharisees were expanding and multiplying their teaching pertaining to angels, so the instruction of both sects was inaccurate.

The suppositions presented in the uninspired writings of the Apocrypha, the Pseudepigrapha, and the other Jewish literature have had great influence on our perception of angels. The information they supply is quite different from the simple, unadorned accounts of angels in Scripture. The Jewish literature of the Talmud and Mishna, as well as the writings of the Essenes must be rejected as sources of information. We discredit the fantasy of Jewish legend and the mystical writings of the Kabbalists as acceptable sources of angelic information.

Instead of attempting to disprove the misinformation of antiquity, each age has added to the distortion. Therefore, it is not surprising that the concept of angels has remained confused through the passage of the ages.

REVIEW

1. How did the Exile affect the future of the Jews?

   _____

2. Can you name four periods of Jewish history?

   _____

3. What was the difference in the Pharisees and the Sadducees? _____

4. What is the name of the Greek translation of Hebrew Scripture? _____

5. When were the apocryphal books written? What is their value? _____

   _____

6. What is the meaning of the word "pseudepigrapha?"

   _____

7. How does the discovery of the Dead Sea Scrolls affect us? _____

8. Discuss the importance of tradition and legend to the Jews. _____

9. What is the Talmud? Mishna? _____

   _____

   _____

NOTES

_____
_____
_____
_____
_____
_____
_____
_____

Chapter Seven

Angels in Art and Literature

T he perception of angels changed and along with the change was a tendency to unquestioningly accept the faulty information as authoritative. For instance, suppose you wanted to draw or paint a representation of an angel. Where would you look for the information you needed? Would you consult the Scriptures, or an art book? Would you draw from the images in your memory? Because images stored in our memories are distorted by centuries of culture and enlightenment, this cannot be considered a reliable source of information.

Neither can the beautiful treasures of art be considered as a dependable way to learn about angels. Artists throughout the ages have made the use of imagination a part of their creative process. Angelic descriptions in the Bible, as we have observed, are somewhat vague. The artists who sought information from Scripture were likely to be disappointed. The biblical descriptions are neither detailed nor plentiful.

VISUAL ART

The existence of art can be documented in every civilization of recorded history. Man has always sought to express his relationship to his surroundings through his art. This art became a reflection of the time and culture in which the artist lived, and was influenced by the period in which he created it.

The appearance of the angel in art takes shape from a combination of Scriptural information, cultural influences, the artist's imagination, and speculation. In a similar manner, we are influenced in our own concept of angels by the accumulation and compounding of misinformation, combined with our own supposition, and an incomplete knowledge of Scripture.

MYTHOLOGY AND ART

Mythology had an extreme influence on our perception of angels. Today we use the term mythology to describe the literature of ancient times which deals with stories of heroes who were elevated to the position of gods. This seems completely harmless, however, the term actually describes the religion of various civilizations which the Bible calls "paganism."

In ancient times man was unable to understand the wonderful workings of God's universe. Mythology began as a system of stories that ancient people invented to explain the entities of nature. To quiet their fears and answer their questions, they invented explanations for all the processes of nature and attributed them all to various gods and goddesses. The solution included imaginary, supernatural persons who caused the sun to rise and set, the crops to grow, and other mysterious things to happen. These characters were deified, becoming the objects of man's worship. Ancient poets such as Homer and Virgil, perpetuated pagan religion by preserving the oral stories about the gods and goddesses of mythology. They gave each of these gods distinct, human characteristics.

You probably never considered the extent to which mythology continues to regulate many parts of our daily lives. For instance, the names of the days of the week, the months, the planets, our country's guided missiles, and many words (flora, fauna, caduceus, cornucopia, Achilles heel) in use today are a result of mythology. The Olympic Games began as a religious festival and featured sacrifices to Zeus, king of the Greek gods.

Many of these details are totally harmless and taken entirely for granted. This era, however, is not blameless in its contribution to our misinformed state regarding heaven's angels. The influence of mythology served to confuse our beliefs concerning angels in indirect ways. Confusion resulted when the artist's depictions of mythological gods and goddesses were so closely akin to their interpretation of angels. The similarity of the representations made the winged goddesses and angels almost inseparable in the minds of men.

There was a complex problem for the artist who wished to portray a spirit being in sculpture or painting. In mythology, the imaginary characters were given human qualities and personality. They were imagined to have human bodies and characteristics. This process is called anthropomorphism. The artists applied the same procedure to angels by imagining them to have mortal bodies and human qualities.

"A picture is worth more than ten thousand words." These familiar words from an old Chinese proverb are very true. However, it is also true that the false impression made by a picture is not erased by ten thousand words. Theology is communicated through the brush of the artist, as well as the pen of the writer, and the spoken word of the teacher. Which is more vividly remembered, what we see, what we read, or what we hear? The visual image is more easily stored and retrieved from memory.

The halo, which has become associated with angels, was adopted from mythology. Originally, the halo was rejected by the artists of Christendom because of its pagan origin. It was not used to exemplify angels until about the fifth century A.D. There is no mention of the halo in scriptural teaching.

We find a strong resemblance in the depiction of Nike, the goddess of victory, and the feminine, beautiful, winged angel. Nike, the ancient Greek goddess of victory, is usually represented as a beautiful, winged woman. A few of these statues which remain are among the most celebrated sculptures in the world today. They bear a confusing resemblance to what artists later interpreted as heavenly angels. A charming, sentimental portrayal of an angel, no matter how inaccurate, may be difficult to dismiss from memory.

JEWISH ART

The Jews were forbidden by law to make representation of heavenly beings in painting or sculpture. This is found in the second of the Ten Commandments,

> You shall not make for yourself an idol in the form of anything in heaven above or on the earth beneath or in the waters below. You shall not bow down to them or worship them; for I, the Lord your God, am a jealous God, punishing the children for the sin of the fathers to the third and fourth generation of those who hate me, but showing love to a thousand generations of those who love me and keep my commandments [Exodus 20:4-6].

This command is responsible for the lack of Jewish paintings and sculpture. It became a dominant theme in Judaism and extended to Islam and some phases of Christianity.

EARLY CHRISTIAN ART

The earliest works of art with a Christian theme are from about 200 A.D. The Roman catacombs were underground burial places of the Christians. Mural type paintings on the walls of these catacombs are among the earliest examples of Christian art. Although very few examples of early Christian art remain today, they portrayed angels in male clothing of the day, without wings, and sometimes with beards. Angels in early Christian art were portrayed with strength and dignity, but later they appeared as sentimental, feminine figures, weighed down with ornate, feathered wings. Underlying this difference in art was a change in the artist's comprehension of angels.

Some manuscripts of the Old Testament contained paintings which were examples of a source of Early Christian art. These were illustrations of the text, made by monks, and were known as illuminated manuscripts or miniatures. This manuscript painting contained ornamental pages, decoration within the text, as well as marginal illustrations. In ancient art the human soul was visualized as a small, winged, nude figure. This reappeared in Early Christian art in the illuminated manuscripts.

There was strong opposition in the early church to the artistic portrayal of individuals considered to be sacred, such as the apostles, Mary, Joseph, etc. These people were later canonized as Saints by the Roman Catholic Church, and declared to be in heaven with God. The decoration of churches with portraits of Christ, paintings of scenes from the Bible, and representation of others considered holy, did not occur until after Constantine's proclamation of Christianity. Rome officially recognized the church in 313 A.D. Almost immediately, many buildings rose in Rome, Constantinople, and throughout the Roman Empire. The walls of these buildings provided large surfaces which the artists were requested to cover with paintings and mosaics.

CLASSICAL ART

The art of ancient Greece was created to decorate the temples of the gods and goddesses. The subjects were the humanlike gods, or scenes from stories about them. In the age of Greek mythology, another purpose of art was to depict history. A successful battle was not only a conquest for the ruler, but also a triumph for the gods. These victories were represented by sculptures of beautiful females with massive wings. The term "Classical art" refers to both Greek and Roman works of art. As the Roman Empire expanded, Classical art spread throughout Europe.

EASTERN ORTHODOX ART

Pictures, but not sculpture were allowed by the Eastern Orthodox Church. By the banning of images, they hoped to avoid idolatry. The art of the East Roman Empire, called Byzantine art, reflected the richness and splendor of the oriental influence and conformed classical art to the requirements of Christianity. Byzantine art primarily depicted biblical characters and scenes. It was known for a particular style which was ornate and made excessive use of gold and rich color. Byzantine art reached its height on the walls of the Eastern Orthodox churches. The spread of Byzantine art and culture to Europe during the Crusades influenced the beginning of the Renaissance.

A traditional decoration in the old Byzantine churches was the Nine Choirs of Angels surrounding the throne of God. The term *choir* signifies a group or division of angels. The idea of an organization of nine grades or ranks of angels is thought to be the result of Jewish teaching concerning different classifications of celestial beings. The Old Testament identifies cherubim, seraphim, and angels. The New Testament speaks of the archangel, thrones, powers, rulers, and authorities. Byzantine artists incorrectly interpreted this as an order or ranking of the heavenly beings.

Classical art was thought to be the peak of man's creative abilities. This era was brought to a sudden end by the destruction of the Roman Empire. In the thousand years that followed the fall of Rome, the Middle Ages, artistic accomplishment was rather insignificant.

MEDIEVAL ART

The art of the Medieval period was complex and not easily defined. Scholarly, religious speculation, under the authority of the Catholic Church was its basis. Distinct, rigid lines, and bizarre, abstract feeling express the Medieval art form. The lack of scale, perspective, and relationship of objects, gives an unrealistic quality to the work of this period. During this time, the use of allegory in religious teaching was popular. Artists expressed truths by symbolic fictional figures and actions. This resulted in the combining of classical myths with Christian belief. Manuscript illumination is the best-preserved and most highly developed art form of the Medieval period. Changes in the Middle Ages, however, did not effect the depiction of angels as feminine, winged, haloed figures.

RENAISSANCE ART

The Renaissance was a period of over three centuries that followed the Middle Ages. It started in Italy about 1400 and spread throughout Europe. This time of "rebirth" saw a revival of all the arts and sciences which prospered in ancient times. It was a time of change, new ideas, and attitudes which still influence our lives today. Artists of this age painted religious figures from biblical history in contemporary surroundings, dressed in current fashions.

Although the Renaissance was a time of great attention to religious art, it was also a time when mythology was reborn. A reawakening of the classic Greek and Roman literature and a revival of pagan attitudes accompanied this renewal of interest in ancient times. Although it was not the primary religious belief of this period, classical mythology was a vital source of inspiration for the artists of Europe for hundreds of years. The painters and sculptors of the Renaissance began to portray mythological characters in their work. The same artists were equally involved in depicting pagan mythology and Christian subjects. One effect of this influence was further confusion of the spiritual angels of heaven with the gods and goddesses of mythology.

The Renaissance artists depicted spiritual angels as human forms with wings, dressed in the fashion of the time. In addition to winged angels, they also painted and sculpted similar winged figures called zephyrs, genii, nymphs, and putti. The *genius* (plural *genii*) was thought to be a spirit assigned to protect a person or a place. The *putto* (plural *putti*) was a fat, winged, nude child, and was included in many paintings of ancient times. They were intended to illustrate various spirits that were thought to be continually present. When the spirit being represented was the spirit of love, it was called a "cupid."

The use of putti was revived in the Early Renaissance when they were thought to represent child angels. These nude, winged children are seen in paintings of mythological as well as religious subjects. They are often mistakenly called "cherubs." This is hardly the likeness of the cherubim which God placed at the Garden of Eden.

> After he drove the man out, he placed on the east side of the Garden of Eden cherubim and a flaming sword flashing back and forth to guard the way to the tree of life [Genesis 3:24].

107

The artists were very often inspired by the Bible and at this time some were commissioned by the Catholic Church to paint and sculpt biblical subjects to illustrate the teachings of the church. It was popular for wealthy families to commission serious works of art to decorate the churches. This was thought to show their generosity and atone for their sins. Very often, angels were included in the paintings regardless of whether angels were mentioned in the particular biblical narrative.

The Annunciation is one of the most popular themes in religious art. These paintings show the angel Gabriel announcing to Mary that she would become the mother of Jesus. Mary is in a domestic setting, dressed not in clothing of biblical times, but in fashions of the artist's day. Mary may be holding needlework, an olive branch, a lily, or a book. Many great artists painted this subject.

Another famous religious subject which was painted by many artists is *Madonna Enthroned*. It depicts Mary on a throne ruling as the queen of heaven. She is holding the Infant Jesus, and is surrounded by angels. The most striking feature of these paintings is the elaborate halos worn by Mary, Jesus, and the angels.

The paintings of the sixteenth century often depicted mythological characters and stories of the gods and goddesses. Many winged figures appear in these creations, hovering overhead or perching on clouds. It is frequently necessary to know the circumstances, the title, or something about the painting, to know whether it is a mythological scene or one from the Bible.

Devotion to the belief in angels was always more pronounced in Catholicism than in Protestantism. However, the absolute acceptance of the doctrine of angels by Protestants is visually affirmed by religious art. The belief survived the Reformation, with its rejections and modifications of Catholic teachings, and remained basic as Protestant churches were established.

The Reformation, however, had a negative effect on art in general. The Catholic Church had been the greatest patron of the artists, but the Protestants discarded religious painting and sculpture. They also rejected the legendary saints and tales of their miracles, which were the subject of the artists' work.

The Counter Reformation of the Catholic Church was an effort to respond to the growing strength of Protestantism. In 1545, The Council of Trent reiterated the beliefs of the Roman Catholic Church and presented a defense against the Reformation. Rules governing the arts were instituted in the final session of 1563. The Council proposed censorship for works that tended to sustain inaccurate doctrines, anything that was not according to strict scriptural interpretation.

LITERATURE

Literature of the Middle Ages and the Renaissance played a significant part in continuing and expanding the misrepresentation of angels. We shall consider only the works of Dante and Milton, although others had a similar part in the resulting confusion. In order to determine their part in this false teaching, we must remember that each of these men and his writing was affected by the culture, religious belief, and philosophy of the time in which he lived.

DANTE

Dante Aligheri was born in Florence, Italy in 1265 and was recognized as the greatest poet of the Middle Ages. Dante was considered a Christian poet. In the historical setting of medieval Europe, the Christian religion was under control of the Catholic Church. The poet of his day was thought to be inspired by God, but in reality, *The Divine Comedy* was a creation of Dante's imagination.

THE DIVINE COMEDY

In the study of Dante's *Divine Comedy*, we see a resemblance to the Book of Revelation. Dante called his poem *Commedia*. Much later, readers added the adjective "divine" to express their feelings of admiration. In his book, the Apostle John related his vision of heaven. Dante's vision included heaven, hell, and purgatory. Purgatory, according to Catholic belief, is the state in which individuals are allowed to atone for sin by suffering before entering heaven. The purpose of Dante's expedition through the afterlife was to give him knowledge to perfect his spiritual state. He was instructed to write what he learned for the benefit of mankind. He wanted to influence the moral character and behavior of the reader, thus, his purpose for writing was edification.

Dante wrote *The Divine Comedy* about 1300. He accepted the *Celestial Hierarchy* of Dionysius as an authoritative source of theological doctrine regarding angels. This was commonly thought to be Dionysius the Areopagite, who was converted by Paul in Athens (Acts 17:34). Paul supposedly related to Dionysius the mysteries of heaven which he had seen when he "was caught up to paradise" (2 Corinthians 12:4). Later, Dionysius was discreditied and became known as Pseudo-Dionysius, which means "False-Dionysius." In the Middle Ages, however, his authority was indisputable.

According to Pseudo-Dionysius the angels were organized into nine ranks from seraphim, the highest, to mere angels, the lowest. Dante illustrated his own acceptance of this belief by representing paradise as being composed of nine circles, layered around a common center. They were classified according to the doctrine of Dionysius: Seraphim, Cherubim, and Thrones; Dominations, Virtues, and Powers; Principalities, Archangels, and Angels.

Dante also represented the structure of hell and purgatory by nine circles. Each circle, or level, of hell was controlled by a character from classical mythology. Dante met a great many notable historical and mythological characters on his journey through these regions. His use of Christian teaching combined with paganism brings about puzzling results. Here was a supposedly Christian poet, writing to warn individuals of the terrors of hell, and he was preoccupied with paganism.

Dante assigned to an angel the duty of transporting souls from hell to purgatory. Dante and his guide stood on the shore and watched as the angel ferried the souls of the saved. Observe that Dante was influenced in his perception of angels by his Catholic training. As they watched him, the angel made the sign of the cross. Dante combined traditional medieval ideas with the symbolism of classical idolatry, and yet the result was called "Divine."

MILTON

John Milton was born in England in 1608. He was a deeply religious man and his beliefs were Protestant. He supported the religious and political endeavors of the Puritans to reform the Church of England. The power of the Puritan Party ended in 1660. At the time he wrote *Paradise Lost*, which was published in 1667, Milton was living in political disfavor and had become totally blind.

Milton believed that the accumulation of knowledge and wisdom were a gift from God. He rejected the ministry and yet believed he, as a poet, had a divine calling. He wrote pamphlets against the priesthood of the Catholic church, proclaiming the rights of the layman. Milton claimed, for all men, equality with the clergy, and the right to speak on spiritual matters. He thought his calling was above that of a Puritan preacher, feeling that his work was inspired of God as that of the prophets.

Milton was a scholar of the Bible and was able to translate the Scriptures. Although he believed literally in the Bible and trusted Scripture above all other sources, he chose to add much information to the scriptural facts concerning the angels of God and the angels of Satan.

He had long sought to write the great English epic and had changed his mind several times about his choice of a subject. When Milton finally chose a theme, it was not one from folklore or legendary history, but from the book of Genesis. Milton selected the subject of the sin of Adam and Eve and their expulsion from the Garden of Eden.

PARADISE LOST

The subject of the epic poem, *Paradise Lost*, is the sin of man and his eviction from Paradise. The study of angels in this work is quite different from that found in the Bible. In addition to a number of angels both good and evil, the characters of this work are God, His Son, Adam, Eve, and Satan.

Paradise Lost consists of twelve books, covering the material presented in the third chapter of Genesis. What was the basis of the additional information which Milton supplied in these thousands of lines of text? He used all the sources of information available to him in mid-seventeenth century. Milton used biblical, classical, medieval, and Renaissance knowledge along with Jewish history and Christian doctrine. He employed fable, myth, and legend as well as knowledge from other fields to accomplish his purpose. His imagination is the fertile ground which produced this enlightenment.

Because *Paradise Lost* covers subject matter which was considered biblical, we may forget that Milton did not limit himself precisely to facts presented by Scripture. Rather, his creative imagination was unlimited in achieving his determined purpose of justifying the ways of God to man. Thus he created undying pictures in our imaginations.

Milton's view of heaven and hell leaves a feeling that they are overpopulated with angels. In all the sixty-nine books of Scripture, only two angels have proper names. A few more are found in the apocryphal books and many in the other literary works. Milton used many of these and derived other angel names from fictional and legendary sources as well.

Milton's angels conformed to the standardized image which was common in that period. They were traditional angels with whom he had become acquainted in the works of art and literature of his period and earlier times. This may indicate a desire to conform to the opinion and persuasion of his contemporaries, but more likely it indicates a lack of investigation and an almost mechanical reproduction of existing views.

The angels of *Paradise Lost* were supplied with the expected halo. Though it was called "tiar," which is crown or "coronet," it was still the glowing circle about the head that the visual arts made an accepted item of angel paraphenalia.

Milton also supplied his angels with wings; Raphael's wings were called "gorgeous." These wings were described as being feathered, even plumed. The wings of Milton's angels, would complicate and impede, rather than promote their movement from place to place.

Although Milton's poem is considered a Christian epic, it is filled with allusion to pagan literature and mythology. Like Dante, Milton was acquainted with The Celestial Hierarchy of Pseudo-Dionysius, and repeatedly used the designations: Thrones, Princedoms, Powers, Dominations, and Virtues when referring to ranks of angels.

The most notable thing about the angels of *Paradise Lost* is their descriptions. On a subject which the Bible allowed to remain mysterious, Milton, with no difficulty, supplied detailed information. It is impossible for most of us to keep the fabrication entirely separate from the reality of Scripture.

Milton was very careful, probably because of his Puritan background, and English tradition, to discreetly portray God the Father and His Son. Yet, he went to great lengths to describe in detail the spirit beings, angels. His imagery was so concrete that it detracts from the mystery which surrounds the angels in Scripture. Milton confused the reader and did the angels a disservice when he endowed them with living bodies, radiant halos, long, flowing hair, and flapping wings.

SUMMARY

Both art and literature are greatly responsible for misinformation about angels which is continually being received as genuine, factual, and true. When a person is exposed to these subjects in the process of education, the lasting result is difficult to remove. If the instructor does not approach the information with a knowledge of Christianity and the Scripture, there is an additional problem for the student. It will be necessary to sort the information to distinguish what, if any, is valid. A student rarely questions the instruction of respected professors.

VISUAL ART SUMMARY

The purpose of the artist throughout history has been to present a faithful representation of his vision. He was never committed to providing a strict interpretation of Scripture. Through his brush, the same artist represented his visions of pagan subjects just as faithfully. Therefore, when we allow the artist to communicate to us a perception of the angels, we are demonstrating our faith in his creative, discovery process. In his attempt to convey a spiritual being painted on canvas, or cut from stone, the artist resorted to such contrivances as the halo, beautiful expression, elaborately draped clothing, and exaggerated wings. Scriptural descriptions are, in comparison, unspecific and somewhat obscure.

We sometimes find the artists' interpretations used to illustrate Scripture. Many Bibles include prints from the works of great artists. When these pictures convey detailed information on angels which is not scriptural, it compounds the problem. Since our memory retains the visual representation more easily than the printed word, our concept of angels becomes further confused.

LITERATURE SUMMARY

Famous works of literature portrayed heaven, hell, and the angels in ways which did not conform to the teachings of Scripture. They were written by religious men with high moral consciousness, but they were fictional accounts of biblical subjects. They contributed to the belief and continuation of the hierarchy or ranking of angels, and erroneous descriptions of angels and their duties.

It is not our purpose to lay blame or find fault with these writers or the literary heritage they have provided. These works have been acclaimed and condemned by many critics over the years. We are not required to decide whether or not they were great writers or if they achieved their purpose. We are not concerned whether Dante and Milton equaled the epics of Homer and Virgil. Our object is to examine these writings for their content on the subject of angels and to determine the effectiveness of their teachings on our understanding of scriptural angels.

Maybe you never read *The Divine Comedy* or *Paradise Lost*. Possibly you never heard of them. You may think that these works of literature have in no way influenced your beliefs. Perhaps you are right. Can you be certain that the commentaries to which you refer were not written by those who were affected by such literature? Are you sure that you have not been taught and directed by those who have accepted this information as a supplement to the Word? The infiltration of this seemingly innocent poetry into teaching on the subject of angels accounts for the perpetuation of beliefs on unsuspecting students and results in a continuation of confusion.

REVIEW

1. How did mythology affect our perception of angels?
   _____

2. What is responsible for the lack of Jewish paintings and sculpture? _____
   _____

3. Early Christian artists portrayed angels as _____
   _____

4. Eastern Orthodox art allowed_____ but prohibited _____

5. Did Medieval art correct the false impressions about angels? _____

6. Why was the Renaissance a time when biblical and mythological influences were combined? _____

7. How did the Renaissance artist portray angels?
   _____

8. Does the cherub in art closely resemble the biblical cherubim? _____

9. Name two writers or their classic literature which contributed to confusion concerning angels. _____
   _____

NOTES

_____
_____
_____
_____
_____
_____

Chapter Eight

False Accusations

C elebrities are often the target of stories which credit them with some accomplishment or characteristic, whether desirable or undesirable, which they do not deserve. Over the years, the angels have also gotten a reputation for some features and abilities which the Scriptures do not attribute to them.

We have filled our minds with poetic descriptions and artistic pictures of romantic, make-believe angels. At the mention of the word, our imaginations produce a mental image based on these picturesque descriptions. The traditional likeness is a human figure with a lovely face; large, feathered wings extending above the shoulder; singing in a beautiful, melodious voice; wearing a flowing garment, with a golden circle above the head.

Where do we find beautiful, winged, singing, haloed angels? The apocryphal books, the pseudepigrapha, and the legends of the Jews are responsible, in part, for this imaginary information. Contributions from mythology, art, and literature are also to blame for the false accusations.

BEAUTIFUL ANGELS?

Beauty is in the eye of the beholder, but we all agree on the meaning of the term "beautiful" as we apply it to our subject. Beauty is physical attractiveness. Can we find reference in Scripture to the charming, delicate beauty we have come to associate with the angel? Some would suggest that King Achish compared David's look with that of an angel, suggesting a charming appearance.

Achish answered, "I know that you have been as pleasing in my eyes as an angel of God; nevertheless the Philistine commanders have said, 'He must not go up with us into battle' " [1 Samuel 29:9].

This was a response to David's request to go and fight the king's enemies. King Achish was not discussing David's looks but was comparing his behavior which was as acceptable as an angel's actions would have been.

Others say the look of Stephen's face, which Luke says was "like the face of an angel," refers to his physical attractiveness.

All who were sitting in the Sanhedrin looked intently at Stephen, and they saw that his face was like the face of an angel [Acts 6:15].

This was hardly the time to begin to describe a good-looking man. False charges had just been brought which would result in Stephen's death and his charming countenance was not an issue.

Emanuel Swedenborg, one of the theological writers who lived between 1688 and 1772, claimed that he had a divine vision and that his writings contained a revelation from God. Swedenborg wrote many volumes of interpretation of the Bible to communicate what he had seen and heard in the world of spirits and angels.

Since angels are men, and live together in society like men on earth, therefore they have garments, houses and other things familiar to those which exist on earth, but, of course infinitely more beautiful and perfect (*The Great Quotations*, by permission of Carole Stuart).

The restraint of the New Testament is in sharp contrast to the exaggeration and detailed information of the apocryphal and pseudepigraphal books. Although they were well-respected in those times, and several of the New Testament writers even quoted from such nonbiblical books, we find their incredibility reinforces our lack of confidence in their authoritativeness.

In the Book of Tobit, an apocryphal book, one of the main characters was an angel called Raphael. He was disguised throughout most of the story as a "beautiful young man." Since the angel in the story and Azarias, the young man he impersonated, were almost interchangeable, this becomes a description of the angel.

Although physical characteristics, such as beauty, are not a part of the scriptural information on angels, Josephus, the Jewish historian of the first century, added some information to the story of Judges 13.

> Now when his wife was once alone, an apparition was seen by her: it was an angel of God, and resembled a young man, beautiful and tall. . .(*Antiquities*, Book V, Chapter VIII].

Josephus contributed a romantic note to the story of the angel's appearance to Samsons' mother. He also commented on some other factors not revealed in Scripture such as her beauty and Manoah's jealousy.

The majority of the responsibility for perceiving the angels to be beautiful lies with the artist's use of mythological beauties in the depiction of angels. Classical statues of the gods and goddesses of Greece and Rome were the models for Renaissance painters and sculptors. These beautiful physical specimens became the accepted manner of illustrating God's angels.

WINGED ANGELS?

The information concerning the movement of angels indicates that they are not limited in their ability to move from place to place as mortals are. In their minds, men confused the descriptions of the heavenly creatures, the cherubim and the seraphim, who have multiple pairs of wings, with the angel's need to travel swiftly. This seemed to be the fastest form of travel to the limited mind of man. So, not realizing the angel's ability to be instantly carried to the places his missions took him, man mentally equipped every angel with a pair of feathered wings.

The use of wings has become indispensable to the portrayal of an angel in art or drama. We find that our intended audience does not understand the illustration or the character to be an angel without the addition of wings. Does the Bible represent the angels as winged beings?

Some of heaven's creatures were indeed described with wings. In fact they had two and three pairs of wings.

> Above him were seraphs, each with six wings: With two wings they covered their faces, with two they covered their feet, and with two they were flying [Isaiah 6:2].

> ... and in the fire was what looked like four living creatures. In appearance, their form was that of a man, but each of them had four faces and four wings [Ezekiel 1:5-6].

> ... and I realized that they were cherubim. Each had four faces and four wings, ... [Ezekiel 10:20b-21a].

> Each of the four living creatures had six wings and was covered with eyes all around, even under his wings. Day and night they never stop saying: "Holy, holy, holy is the Lord God Almighty, who was, and is, and is to come" [Revelation 4:8].

These creatures, however, are not the conventional angel messengers of God, but they are heavenly creatures in addition to the angels.

We do find two verses of Scripture which speak of angels and flying, but the first seems to refer to speed rather than winged flight as we think of it.

> ... while I was still in prayer, Gabriel, the man I had seen in the earlier vision, came to me in swift flight about the time of the evening sacrifice [Daniel 9:21].

The term which is translated "swift flight" literally means "with weariness," as one who is tired from running.

The other verse is found in the apocalyptic Book of Revelation and it does mean "to fly."

> Then I saw another angel flying in midair, and he had the eternal gospel to proclaim to those who live on the earth to every nation, tribe, language and people [Revelation 14:6].

The word "flying" in this verse does mean winged flight, even feathered, winged flight. This particular word, however, is used only in the Book of Revelation. We know this book describes a symbolic vision. Revelation 12:14 portrays a woman with the wings of an eagle, but this is not to be interpreted literally.

The King James Version has one more reference to a flying angel. The word "angel" in this verse is somewhat doubtful because the word "eagle," appears in some of the oldest manuscripts.

> And I beheld, and heard an angel flying through the midst of heaven, saying with a loud voice, Woe, woe, woe, to the inhabiters of the earth by reason of the other voices of the trumpet of the three angels, which are yet to sound [Revelation 8:13] KJV.

> As I watched, I heard an eagle that was flying in midair call out in a loud voice: "Woe! Woe! Woe to the inhabitants of the earth, because of the trumpet blasts about to be sounded by the other three angels!" [Revelation 8:13].

Bible scholars think that this was possibly the error of a copyist. The eagle was the symbol of the Roman Empire and would represent judgment descending from above as the bird of prey attacking its victims.

To summarize the scriptural information: 1. We have found a description of wings on some heavenly creatures, but not on angel messengers. 2. There is a verse which refers to flight, but does not imply winged flight. 3. Another verse does mean fly as the flight of birds but cannot be interpreted literally. 4. Finally, a verse which refers to an angel flying, but it should read eagle flying. This seems to be a very weak case for attaching cumbersome, feathered wings to our mental image of an angel.

Apart from the scriptural information on the winged flight of angels is the contribution from other sources. In ancient times, the means of transport for angels was imagined to be flying. The only form of flight available to the mind of these people was the soaring of the birds. The word *fledge* means, to acquire the feathers necessary for flight. This describes the way they must have felt about the angels, i.e. angels must have feathers to have the ability to fly.

There is a view which is popular in modern literature and drama that angels earn their wings. The origin of this theory is uncertain. One explanation is that the seraphim, which are closest to the throne, have the most wings. Therefore, the idea that it would be desirable to have more wings. From that perhaps the thought that they could be earned.

The Greeks believed their gods and goddesses were winged, and they believed their souls would ascend with wings at death. But more than anything else, they believed that the ones that were messengers between the gods and the mortals had to have wings.

The tales of mythology are far more fantastic and bizarre than anything written by science fiction authors, yet they were not considered fabrication, or fantasy, but believed to be theology. Although the gods and goddesses of Mount Olympus are no longer worshipped and revered, they continue to have an effect on our lives today.

The messenger of the Greek gods was Hermes. He wore a winged cap and wings on his shoes. He was the messenger to mortals. His name means "hastener," which suggests the speed of the messenger. The swift messenger of the Roman gods was Mercury who wore wings on his hat and sandals. Ancient people were taught by Greek religion that communication with the gods was through sacred messengers.

Rembrandt painted a series of canvases illustrating the story of Tobias and the angel from the apocryphal Book of Tobit. The use of wings is so necessary to the portrayal of an angel in art, that in every scene Raphael was a winged figure. Although he had taken the form of a man and Tobias did not realize he was an angel, Rembrandt found it necessary to resort to the use of wings.

The Secrets of Enoch, or 2 Enoch, a pseudepigraphal book, written during the intertestamental period, is supposed to be the story of Enoch's translation and ascent into the heavens. From this record we read:

> It came to pass, when Enoch had told his sons, that the angels took him on their wings and bore him up on to the first heaven and placed him on the clouds (2 Enoch III).

They brought before my face the elders and rulers of the stellar orders, and showed me two hundred angels who rule the stars and their services to the heavens, and fly with their wings and come round all those who sail (2 Enoch IV).

And I looked and saw other flying elements of the sun, whose names are Phoenixes and Chalkydri, marvelous and wonderful, with feet and tails in the form of a lion, and a crocodile's head, their appearance is empurpled, like the rainbow; their size is nine hundred measures, their wings are like those of the angels, each has twelve... (2 Enoch XII:1).

...and spirits and elements and angels flying; each angel has six wings (2 Enoch XIX:7).

Jewish legend tells of an angel called Ben Nez the Winged who has the job of keeping the south wind back with his wings, so that the world will not be consumed by its heat.

Another story from Jewish legend which shows the typical means of angelic travel is the story of the archangel Michael visiting Abraham to bring him the message of death. When Michael returned,

Spreading out his wings, he rose speedily to Heaven there to join the choir of ministering angels who daily assemble before the Throne of Glory at sunset to sing the praises of the Eternal (*Ancient Israel: Myths and Legends*, I:325).

The association of the angel and wings has become so firmly established that the wing is the symbol of the angel. In signing for the deaf, the interpreter expresses the word "angel" by touching the shoulders and then flapping the hands as if they were a pair of wings.

SINGING ANGELS?

"Good night sweet prince; and flights of angels sing thee to thy rest!" This is a familiar quotation, but it is not biblical. It is Horatio speaking at the time of Hamlet's death (William Shakespeare, *Hamlet*, Act V, Scene II.) The word "sing" means to produce musical tones by means of the voice, but it also means to relate or celebrate something in verse or to compose poetry. Therefore it is necessary to understand how we are using the word "sing." We are now considering the voicing of words in a pleasant arrangement of sounds with musical quality and tone. Please make a mental or a written note at this time to remind you of your concept of angelic song. Do you equate angels singing with perhaps the Mormon Tabernacle Choir performing the *Hallelujah Chorus*?

The angels have a language of their own and we know that they praise God, but we do not find that Scripture supports our impression of the singing of angels in exquisite voices.

> If I speak in the tongues of men and of angels, but have not love, I am only a resounding gong or a clanging symbol [1 Corinthians 13:1].

> Praise the Lord, you his angels, you mighty ones who do his bidding, who obey his word. Praise the Lord, all his heavenly hosts, you his servants who do his will [Psalm 103:20-21].

There are some who say that a passage in Job with which we have already become familiar, refers to angels singing.

> . . . while the morning stars sang together and all the angels shouted for joy? [Job 38:7].

Actually, it says the sons of God shouted. The term used here is usually interpreted "angels." Regardless of what the morning stars were, we are told that the sons of God, which were the angels, shouted not sang.

If you were searching for a passage that tells of angels singing, where would you look first? Perhaps you would think of the occasion when the angels appeared to the shepherds.

> Suddenly a great company of the heavenly host appeared with the angel, praising God and saying, "Glory to God in the highest, and on earth peace to men on whom his favor rests" [Luke 2:13-14].

Notice that the angels were "praising God and saying" not singing. This is true for all the translations in general use today except the New English Version which says sing. The Greek word which is used here is *lego* which means to say, speak, or affirm.

There is one verse which is translated "sing" and refers to angels. This translation appears only in the New International and the New English Versions. In the following passage, the Greek words which are translated "sang" and "singing" in the New International and English Versions are translated "said" and "saying" in other versions, including King James and American Standard. Although this Greek word can be used to mean "sing," it is translated "say" in other Scripture references.

> Then I looked and heard the voice of many angels, numbering thousands upon thousands, and ten thousand times ten thousand. They encircled the throne and the living creatures and the elders. In a loud voice they sang: "Worthy is the Lamb, who was slain, to receive power and wealth and wisdom and strength and honor and glory and praise!" Then I heard every creature in heaven and on earth and under the earth and on the sea, and all that is in them, singing: [Revelation 5:11-13a].

This is an unfortunate interpretation and the translators took liberty to do so. Elsewhere the Greek word *lego* is never translated "sing" in the Bible.

It is possible that a part of our confusion concerning the singing of angels results from our conception of the word praise. The angels praise God, and our idea of the ultimate praise is a beautiful voice calling forth to God in song.

In the first century, however, it probably was not so beautiful. History tells us that primitive vocal music was mostly noise. In the early church the music was not developed into the art form it has become today. History says that the music of the Hebrews was called "divine service, not art." Most of their music was secondary to recitation, and "it was unharmonic, simple and inclined to be coarse and noisy" (Edward Dickinson, *Music in the History of the Church*, 1969).

Although the people who had a Jewish background would have been accustomed to instruments of music in their Temple worship, the music of the synagogue was a cappella. There is no record of musical instruments in Christian worship for the first 600 years. The people expressed their feelings to God in chants and recitations. There was no harmony, as we sing today, in four or more parts until the eleventh century. This musical form became fully-developed in the latter half of the sixteenth century.

What was the quality of angelic music as they first began to praise God? Did their skill, ability, and training get better in the same way human music has improved? We have now excelled to a level far superior to first century Christian singing. Have the angels also improved their degree of proficiency in singing?

Surely you see how ridiculous this is. The angels were created by God and given abilities to praise Him. Their capability is so far superior to our singing that the Scripture does not even use the word "sing" with reference to angels. Does this mean they cannot sing? Certainly not! But, if they do, the Scripture does not provide us with this information.

There is a variety of supposition about the songs of angels. The ancient Jewish view of angelic music said that the angels do not repeat their song and that when they have sung they disappear, and another, that the angels sing only at night when the songs of the Jews have ceased. There is also the speculation that the degree of sweetness of the angels' songs is determined by how fervently and sincerely the earthly voices sing (The Encyclopaedia Judaica Jerusalem).

In Milton's *Paradise Lost*, the angel's sang praises to the Son of God (Book III:365-71). Adam told Eve that if they listened carefully, they could hear the angels singing (Book IV). Raphael told Adam that God sent His Son to create the world while the angels celebrated with the singing of hymns (Book V).

The pseudepigraphal book of 2 Enoch includes many references to the singing of angels, as well as cherubim and seraphim.

> ... and inexpressible singing of the host of Cherubim, and of the boundless light (2 Enoch I:1).

> ... in their midst are six Phoenixes and six Cherubim and six six-winged ones continually with one voice singing one voice, and it is not possible to describe their singing... (2 Enoch XIX:3).

One thing which reinforces our tendency to think of singing angels is the wording of some of our beautiful hymns. As we sing these hymns, we are caused repeatedly to experience the concept of singing angels.

ANGELIC HALO?

The halo, which has become associated with angels, was adopted from mythology. Another term for halo is *nimbus*. The halo, or nimbus, is supposed to surround the head of a divine person to signify spiritual character through the symbolism of light. According to mythology, a radiant light surrounded the heads of gods and goddesses when they came down from Mount Olympus. In Greek and Roman art, the halo was adopted to set apart the human-like gods and goddesses from the mortals. It was later used by artists to distinguish the Roman emperors.

Because it originated in paganism, it was at first rejected by early Christian artists. About the middle of the fourth century, however, the circle of light was used in depicting Christ. It was used in representing angels about the fifth century, but was not commonly used for Mary until the sixth century.

Although there is no mention of the halo in Scripture, it gradually came into use and by the Middle Ages was accepted practice in portraying Jesus, angels, and saintly mortals. The halo found its way to India with the Greek invaders and began to appear in Buddhist art about the end of the third century.

The halo is not a teaching of Scripture and this verse from John's vision does not describe the angels' halo as a rainbow.

Then I saw another mighty angel coming down from heaven. He was robed in a cloud, with a rainbow above his head; his face was like the sun, and his legs were like fiery pillars [Revelation 10:1].

At first the halo was just an unadorned circle of light, but it was thought necessary to supplement this by adding to the halos of some such as, Christ, the apostles, and others. The halo of Christ was sectioned by the addition of a cross. Matthew's halo was shown with an angel placing a scroll on it, to illustrate the inpsiration of the Gospel. The halo being touched by an angel was an illustration of a writer's inspiration by God.

In Catholic teaching, the halos are symbolic. They appear incredible and absurd, but they are believed to impart complex benefits. Eventually some of the halos were ornamented with jewels and artists added rays to make them even more conspicuous.

SUMMARY

Angels are the object of false accusations which cannot be substantiated by Scripture. They are charged with having physical attractiveness, outrageous, feathered wings, an astonishing ability to sing, and an ever-present, always-glowing halo. These unnecessary impediments were bestowed on the angels by tradition, but have now become accepted by many people. Belief in beautiful, winged, singing, haloed angels is not the product of a study of the Scriptures. Although these details seem desirable to us, they would only restrict and hinder the performance of an angel.

The apocryphal, pseudepigraphal, and theological writings supplied detailed information which is in marked contrast with the restraint of the New Testament. The use of mythological models by the painters and sculptors in ancient times was responsible for much of the confusion people experienced concerning the loveliness of the angels. Since an extensive amount of this work continues to be available to us today, the problem it created continues. Biblical descriptions, however, do not depict angels as beautiful or attractive creatures.

Although the Scriptures describe wings on some heavenly creatures, this is not an element of angel messengers. Verses which refer to the flight of angels seem to imply haste rather than winged flight.

There are many Bible verses which teach of singing, but they do not refer to the singing of angels. We imagine that praise and singing are equivalent expressions. There is no reason to restrict the praise of angels to human limits. We are taught by the lyrics of many of our favorite hymns that angels sing.

The halo is a product of mythology and originated in paganism. The first response of Christian artists was to reject it for this reason. The halo was used to depict holy subjects by the symbol of light. A simple circle of light was later glaringly exaggerated. There is nothing in Scripture which corresponds to the angelic halo.

We must examine our perception of God's messengers to learn if our understanding comes from the Scripture or from some uninspired source. We must also be willing to correct the false mental images which we have. This can be accomplished by a study of the Scriptures.

REVIEW

1. Name four attributes which are falsely ascribed to angels. _____

2. Several sources of information contributed to this confusion. How many can you name? _____

3. Which source is primarily responsible for our perception that angels are beautiful?_____

4. According to the Bible, which heavenly creatures have wings? _____

5. How does the hymn book contribute to the belief that angels sing? _____

6. Describe music in the early church._____

7. Why did Christian artists originally reject the halo?
   _____

8. What was the purpose of the halo in mythological art?
   _____

   In religious art? _____

9. How may we correct our perception of angels, if a misconception exists?_____
   _____

NOTES

_____
_____
_____
_____
_____
_____
_____
_____
_____
_____
_____
_____
_____
_____
_____
_____
_____
_____
_____
_____
_____
_____
_____

Chapter Nine

Angels and Other Religions

A study of angels usually includes only the teachings of Judaism and Christianity. There are, however, other religions which believe that intermediary spirits act as messengers of their gods. These teachings of the spirit world in ancient times may have effected the perception of God's angels which has been passed on to us.

Every religious belief has a history of doctrine which perpetuates faith in its followers. The more we learn about their doctrines, the more variation we see between them and the Scripture. In most religions, there is a belief in some sort of spirit beings both favorable and hostile. The Eastern religions assigned the service performed by angels to spirit beings who were extensions of their multiple gods. In some of these religions, there is also a neutral spirit which is capable of good or bad.

HINDUISM

The native religion of India is Hinduism. Hinduism reaches from 1500 B.C. to the present. It is said to be the oldest religion now in existence. Various levels of Hindu were represented by many gods, but about 250 B.C. they began to subordinate their gods and goddesses in favor of a move toward monotheism. These lesser gods were not abolished but became equivalent in function to the angels of Christianity. In Hindu belief, the intermediary spirits were called *devas*. The evil opposition of the devas was the *asuras* or demons. The sacred writing was called the *Veda* and it was written in Sanskrit.

A majority of the people of India are of the Hindu religion, which is made up of a number of different divisions and beliefs. The principal teachings of this body are the caste system of social classification, a form of meditation called yoga, and a belief in reincarnation.

Reincarnation for the Hindu is not the alluring idea of life again that has been presented to us. For him it is a belief that he will continue to be born and reborn, endlessly — again, and again, and again. The ultimate goal is to reach perfection or salvation and escape from the continuing process.

BUDDHISM

Buddhism denies the existence of an eternal supreme being who is the creator of the world. Instead, it advocates acceptance of a large number of temporary gods, to whom believers appeal for assistance and protection. *Buddha* is the title first given to Siddhartha Guatama. He was the original in a series of "Enlightened Ones." Gautama lived in India in the sixth century B.C. and his teachings began as a reform movement of Hinduism. He was opposed to the caste system. He did not, however, reject the belief in reincarnation or attempt to modify the acceptance of the collection of gods that were revered in India.

The Buddhist practice of meditation attempts to release one from the recurring cycle of birth and rebirth through attaining Nirvana. Nirvana is associated with peace and tranquility, and is a state of bliss which results from the extinction of desire.

There was no written record of Buddha's teaching, so his words were passed down orally by his followers. His revelation teaches of men who become gods (buddhas). This great collection of Buddhist gods has a similar role to that of the angels of Christian belief. These favorable spirits of Buddhist belief were designated as *devas*. The Buddhist appealed to lesser gods, angels, or other intermediaries for assistance and preservation. There was, however, no evidence of spirit messengers in their teaching.

Buddhist art maintained the use of the halo which was a product of classical mythology. In paintings of the seventh century A.D. the figure of Buddha is shown with celestial attendants which resemble the hovering, winged infants of Christian art in the Renaissance Period.

ZOROASTRIANISM

The Zoroastrian religion teaches the existence of beings called *amesha spentas* who are go-betweens for the human followers and their god. Zoroaster was born in Persia, which is now Iran, about 600 B.C. He became a prophet and the founder of the Zoroastrian religion. This was the principal pre-Islamic religion of Iran. The strongest feature of this Iranian doctrine was the teaching of dualism. This is the belief that good and evil powers are both supreme and existed from eternity.

The sacred writing of the Zoroastrians is the *Avesta*. The oldest part is thought to have been written by Zoroaster himself. In this religious writing, there was a dramatic competition between the Beneficent Spirit and the Destructive Spirit. Zoroaster called the good power Ahura Mazda, and the evil force he called Ahriman. In spite of his dualistic leanings, Zoroaster always hated the evil power and taught that Ahura Mazda and his angels of light would be the final victors.

Zoroaster taught that the six sons and daughters of Ahura Mazda are the *amesha spentas* or the "Bounteous Immortals." Through them Ahura Mazda received praise and gave rewards and punishments. They have been compared to archangels. Other heavenly beings were the *yatzas*, the Adorable or Worshipful Ones. They were said to be innumerable and similar to the angels of Christianity.

There were also beings called *devas*, which were evil spirits. Notice this was the name given to good spirits by Hinduism and Buddhism. In Zoroastrian belief, however, they were a countless group of demons whose responsibility was to prevent a proper relationship between Ahura Mazda and man. The devas were used by Ahriman, the evil one, to lead man astray and cause him to make improper choices. This resulted in the punishment of man in a chasm of fire.

Zoroaster maintained that he was taken to heaven where he was allowed to see God. One of the amesha spentas, the archangel Vohu Manah, nine times larger than a man, told Zoroaster to leave his body and follow him to Ahura Mazda and his angels, who were characterized by extreme brightness.

Zoroaster supposedly had six celestial visions, in which the archangels or "Bounteous Immortals" instructed him. He supplied each archangel with character attributes which personified special values. In each vision, a specific archangel informed him about the particular duties which were in the realm of that angel's responsibility.

Zoroaster's teachings stressed four points:
Worship Ahura Mazda   Marry your nearest relative.
Magnify the Archangels.   Damn the demons.
(Charles Francis Potter, *Great Religious Leaders*).

For the first twelve years that he preached, Zoroaster had little or no success. The turning point was when he converted King Vishtaspa, a powerful ruler east of Persia. An old account of their meeting says that Zoroaster taught the religion to Vishtaspa through the use of various methods including "the presentation of the visible testimony of the archangels."

The Jews were taken into captivity by the Babylonians three years before Zoroaster died. In 536 B.C., Babylon was conquered by Cyrus King of Persia. Cyrus was a Zoroastrian and did much to spread this religion. His reputation for generosity to the Jews may have resulted from his faith in the religion of Zoroaster. Historians believe that the humanitarian principles of the Zoroastrians were a strong influence on the Jews. It is also likely that the Zoroastrian beliefs concerning the spirit world made an impression on Judaism.

ISLAM

Islam is the fastest growing religion in the United States today. Belief in angels is a basic part of Islamic teaching. Although Moslem beliefs are quite unlike those of Christians, their teaching relating to angels is similar to the Bible. Only two angels are named in their sacred writing, the *Koran*. They are the same two named in Scripture, Gabriel and Michael.

Islam began as a reform of Judaism, and has become the faith of eight hundred million of the world's population, two million of whom live in the United States. This means that there are as many Moslems in this country as there are Episcopalians.

In 610 A.D., a man named Mohammed, about forty years of age, went into a cave outside Mecca to meditate. He claimed that the angel Gabriel appeared to him in a dream, called him to be a prophet, and gave him words which would later be a part of the Koran. Islam teaches that Jesus, like Mohammed, was a prophet, and strongly denies that He is the Son of God.

In later revelations, Gabriel is supposed to have communicated the entire contents of the Koran to Mohammed. Bits and pieces of the Koran were written down by his followers from time to time. It was not until after Mohammed's death that the fragments were assembled and the Koran was put in a permanent form.

The religion preached by Mohammed is called Islam, and those who follow these teachings are called Moslems. This is from the Arabic word *Muslim* which means "one who submits." Though the Moslems refer to Him as "Allah," they claim to worship God.

Mohammed did not think of himself as the author of a new religion, but a reformer of the Jews. The Jews, however, were not anxious to convert and the Moslems were not very successful. Allah, through Gabriel, then presumably told Mohammed to attack the unbelievers. To guarantee the support of Moslems in these evangelistic battles, Mohammed promised great rewards for the victorious and immediate entry into Paradise for those who were killed. Since the Moslems were often triumphant, this method produced large numbers of converts.

The promise of immediate entrance into Paradise, without waiting for the Judgment, was made even more attractive to the warriors by Islamic teaching. They believed that Paradise was a place of endless sensual pleasure where the Moslem would be enthroned, surrounded by beautiful women, and supplied with special food and drink.

Mohammed taught that those who were judged evil would be punished by the angels. For instance, the Archangel Malik would clothe the wicked with fiery clothing, beating them with clubs of iron, and compel them to drink boiling water.

Although the Koran names only Gabriel and Michael, Moslem tradition includes two more angels: Azrail and Israfil. Gabriel was the messenger of Allah who came to Mohammed. Michael is believed to command the forces of nature. Azrail is the Angel of Death who takes away a person's last breath. Israfil is believed to be the one who will blow the trumpet at the time of Judgment.

Moslems believe that the Five Pillars of Islam are the most important commands of Allah.

One Pillar states:

Belief: In Allah, the only God; in the prophets; in Mohammed the final and greatest prophet; in the Last Judgment; and in angels, the messengers of God (Leonard F. Hobley, *Moslems and Islam*).

The primary function of angels in Islam is to praise Allah, serve Allah, and do the will of Allah. Their foremost task is messenger, but they are also seen as Allah's throne bearers, guardians of the gates of Paradise and Hell, and intercessors with God for men.

Islam also recognizes spiritual beings in addition to angels which were called *djinni*, or genies. They seem to have some characteristics in common with angels. First, the genies may be either good or evil, visible or invisible, and capable of assuming the form of man or animal. According to tradition, they were created from fire two thousand years before Adam.

The teaching of Islam recognizes demons which contend for the control of men's lives. The chief among these is Iblis (the Devil), who tempts mortal man. Iblis is the Islamic name for Lucifer, whom they claim was cast out of heaven for rebellion against God, becoming Satan, the Tempter.

One night angels came and prepared Mohammed for a journey through Paradise. According to legend, Gabriel awakened the prophet and purified him, filling his soul with faith and wisdom. Then Mohammed rode on a composite animal which resembled a mule with the tail of a peacock. He was supposedly allowed to ride through seven heavens and privileged to look on the face of God.

Mohammed opposed idolatry, including statues of religious persons as well as their representation in painting. Later, however, this was ignored and Islamic art was created by leaving the face of Mohammed unpainted. One such work depicts Mohammed's journey to paradise, with Gabriel as his guide. The painting is called *The Ascension of Mohammed.* The prominent features of this painting are the fiery halos behind Mohammed and Gabriel and Mohammed's face, which is completely blank.

The most sacred shrine of Islam is called the *Kaaba.* According to tradition, the angel Gabriel brought an unusual black stone to Abraham. Abraham, with Ishmael's help, is said to have built the original home of this stone which became the Kaaba. The Kaaba is a small building of the Great Mosque of Mecca. Set in the south wall of this building is a Black Stone encircled in silver. When Moslems pray, they turn their faces toward Mecca and the Kaaba. Reaching the Kaaba is the goal of the Moslems who make a pilgrimage to Mecca.

DIVERGENT CHRISTIAN GROUPS

A wide variation of teaching concerning angels exists among those who profess a belief in Christ. The two groups which we shall consider next claim to believe in Jesus Christ, and accept the Bible as the sacred Word of God. The problem of their misinformation about angels stems from translations and interpretations as well as additions to Scripture. The groups have used these methods to support their doctrine, thus contributing to confusion concerning angels.

LATTER-DAY SAINTS

The Church of Jesus Christ of Latter-day Saints does not limit its doctrine and beliefs to the Word of God as revealed in the canonical books of the Bible. They accept The Book of Mormon, Doctrine and Covenants, and The Pearl of Great Price as inspired literature. In addition to these books, the current Latter-day Saints prophet is believed to receive communication from God for the church.

The Book of Mormon is a volume which they believe was recorded by Mormon in ancient times. The information was inscribed on metal plates and hidden by Moroni, who was Mormon's son. They maintain that in fulfillment of Revelation 14:6-7, Moroni, who had become an angel, returned and revealed the plates to Joseph Smith. He received the golden plates in 1827.

The information contained in these records is said to relate God's dealings with the American continents from 2247 B.C. to 421 A.D. According to this book, Mormon was a prophet who led the Lehi people to America in 600 B.C. Moroni added the records of the Jaredites who had already settled in America. They were supposed to have come here after the scattering of peoples and the confusion of language when the attempt to build the tower of Babel failed. They claim the remnant of these tribes is the American Indians. They also maintain that Jesus came to America and appeared to these people after His resurrection.

The Latter-day Saint's doctrine teaches beliefs concerning angels which are foreign to the teaching of Scripture. For instance, Raphael, Michael, and Gabriel are believed by Latter-day Saints to have come to earth in the present age. The purpose of this visitation was to administer powers called "keys" to Joseph Smith.

They believe in different types of beings who serve as angels: Latter-day Saints assert that one kind of angel is called a "pre-existent spirit." Before a person is born on earth, his spirit lives with God. He is a spirit-child of God, and therefore, deity. In the pre-existent state, the angel is trained and educated to act for God when he receives mortal life.

Latter-day Saints doctrine concerning pre-existence and the angels, identifies the first man, Adam, as the pre-existent angel, Michael. It is taught that three years before

Adam died, he called his descendants together to bless them, and they called him Michael the archangel (Doctrine and Covenants 107:53-54).

Noah is said to have been the angel Gabriel before he was on earth as a mortal. The angel Raphael, from the apocryphal Book of Tobit, they speculate to have been Enoch.

Another angelic category in this belief is a "translated being." The translated beings were righteous people in ancient times, who did not die but were taken to heaven. Following their translation they became angels. As angels they are said to have appeared on earth and ministered to people. They say the apostle John was a translated being (Doctrine and Covenants 7).

The next group of angels, according to the Latter-day Saints, is the "spirits of just men made perfect." These are the spirits of those who are saved and await the resurrection.

Another group of angels, as taught by the Latter-day Saints, is called "resurrected personages." The resurrected personages "were with Christ in his resurrection," and became angels (Doctrine and Covenants 133:55). A resurrected personage has a physical body in heaven for the purpose of coming back to earth to give messages or special power to certain men (Doctrine and Covenants 129).

According to Latter-day Saints teaching, Moroni returned to earth as a "resurrected personage" and gave the plates to Joseph Smith. Smith, they say, was miraculously able to translate these ancient records by the use of two special stones. These stones, the Urim and the Thummim, were provided to Smith by the angel Moroni. The translation he made was published in 1830 as a supplement to the Scripture.

The myth that Satan was an angel who sinned is taught by the Latter-day Saints. In addition to the sources referred to in Chapter 13, "Evil Angels," you may also note this one from the Book of Mormon.

And I, Lehi, according to the things which I have read, must needs suppose that an angel of God, according to that which is written, had fallen from heaven; wherefore, he became a devil, having sought that which was evil before God. And because he had fallen from heaven, and had become miserable forever, he sought also the misery of all mankind (2 Nephi 2:17-18a).

JEHOVAH'S WITNESSES

Jehovah's Witnesses take their name from Isaiah 43:12, ". . .Ye are my witnesses, saith Jehovah, and I am God" (American Standard Version). Although this group claims Abel as its first member, Charles T. Russell actually established the movement in approximately 1886. Witnesses have placed an interpretation on biblical facts which produces an altered view of angels. They also claim to receive the inspired word of God today, through invisible angels.

The sect is directed by the Watch Tower Bible and Tract Society, which was incorporated in 1884. The *Watchtower* magazine is the organization's means of transmitting information to its members. This publication was first printed in 1897. The *1939 Yearbook of Jehovah's Witnesses*, claimed that the *Watchtower* is God's means of communicating with man on earth today. It further stated that *"The Watchtower* has published in each issue some further enlightenment of Jehovah's prophecies." The method of this inspiration is through invisible angels who bring the instructions from God to the witnesses.

The Watchtower of December 15, 1987 contains an article titled, "ANGELS Do They Affect Your Life?" Under the heading "How Do Angels Affect You?," we find the claim that the 3,000,000 Jehovah's Witnesses who proclaim the "message" are assisted by angels. They maintain that they are "angel-directed," in reaching those who will accept their teaching. The topic, "Angels in Your Future," states that a person's future depends on how he responds to "angelic direction," and the "angelically backed message" (*The Watchtower,* "Angels in Your Future," Vol. 108, No. 24, 6,7).

This sect opposes the deity of Christ and asserts that He existed in heaven as the archangel Michael before He came to earth to live as the Son of Mary. They teach that

Jesus (Michael) was the first angel created by God. Further, they allege that the resurrected Jesus resumed the identity of Michael after ascending to heaven. Attempting to prove these claims, they cite Scriptures which show similarities linking Jesus and angels.

First there is the name; Jesus is the Son of God and angels were called "sons of God" in Job 1:6, 2:1. Then there is the fact that Jesus, the Messiah, is called "the messenger of the covenant" in Malachi 3:1, and the word angel means messenger. Genesis 3:15 told that the seed of woman would bruise the head of Satan, and 1 John 3:8 named Jesus as the one to destroy the works of Satan. Yet, Revelation 12:7 said Michael fought against Satan in the war in heaven.

In the Revelation of John, some of the angels were presented to John in various situations in which Jesus was also depicted. For instance, Jesus was called the "Lion of the tribe of Judah" (Revelation 5:5), and the angel in Revelation 10:3 had a "shout like the roar of a lion." Matthew 17:2 described Jesus at the transfiguration, "His face shown like the sun" (also Revelation 1:16). The angel in Revelation 10:1 also resembled this description, "his face was like the sun." John described the feet of Jesus in Revelation 1:15, "His feet were like bronze glowing in a furnace." In Revelation 10:1, the angel is described, "his legs [feet (KJV)] were like fiery pillars." The descriptions are similar—"glowing" or "fiery."

Jehovah's Witnesses claim these and other parallels and similarities indicate that Jesus returned to heaven as an angel, Michael. Their belief does not deny that Jesus is the Son of God, but rejects Him as deity. They do not accept the three persons in one Godhead, believing that the Trinity was originated by the Catholic church.

The Witnesses teach that the devil was created a good angel who later sinned and became Satan. In the book *You Can Live Forever in Paradise on Earth*, Chapter Two is called, "An Enemy of Everlasting Life." In this context, the subject of the identity of the devil is considered. They conclude that an angel of God made himself the devil. The narration goes on to tell how this rebellious angel made a serpent seem to speak to Eve. He lied to her and by doing this he became the enemy of God or a Satan.

SUMMARY

The oldest surviving religious beliefs in spirit beings have little resemblance to God's angels. It is therefore interesting to consider whether these doctrines have contributed to our own misunderstanding. The teachings of Hindus and Buddhists are of multiple gods and goddesses which may have functioned as intermediaries but do not have similarity to the angels of Scripture.

The Jews were exposed to Zoroastrian beliefs while they were captives in Babylon and after their return from captivity. They were influenced at this time to begin the enhancement of the simple information of the Bible concerning angels. A knowledge of the Islamic belief in angels shows them to be comparable to biblical angels in many of their functions.

The teachings of the Latter-day Saints would seem to contribute to the confusion concerning the origin, nature, and function of angels as they are revealed to us in the Bible. Jehovah's Witnesses also add to the misinformation which is prevalent concerning the angels. These two groups also happen to be the ones who are most active in "doorstep ministries." Thus, their opinions become more widespread.

REVIEW

1. In what country did the Hindu religion originate?

_____

2. What religion was considered a reform of Hinduism?

_____

3. What religious teaching had the most influence on the Jews? _____

4. What is the name of the Islamic prophet?_____

5. Give another name for the Islamic religion. _____

_____

6. Name the sacred books of the LDS in addition to the Bible. _____

_____

7. Name the categories of angels taught by the Latter-day Saints which are not found in Scripture.

_____

_____

8. What present day angelic activities are taught by Jehovah's Witnesses? _____

_____

9. What is taught by Jehovah's Witnesses concerning the angel Michael? _____

_____

NOTES

_____

_____

_____

_____

_____

_____

_____

_____

_____

_____

_____

_____

_____

_____

_____

_____

_____

_____

_____

_____

_____

_____

_____

_____

_____

Chapter Ten

The Angel of the Lord

Although we do not read much about the activities of Jesus during the time of the Old Testament, we know that He was with God from the very beginning.

> In the beginning was the Word, and the Word was with God, and the Word was God [John 1:1].

> Father, I want those you have given me to be with me where I am, and to see my glory, the glory you have given me because you loved me before the creation of the world [John 17:24].

What was Jesus doing at this time? Was He in heaven, just waiting until God sent Him to earth to live a human life? Or did He have a more significant role, acting for God by representing Him as the angel of the Lord.

ANGEL OF THE LORD

There was one angel in the Bible who was truly unique. He spoke for God, required reverence, made promises in the Name of God, forgave sins, and revealed the future. He is the being who was called "the angel of the Lord." This angel was mentioned throughout the Old Testament. The American Standard Version calls him "the angel of Jehovah." There are also references in the King James Version of the New Testament to the angel of the Lord, but they would be more correctly translated "an angel of the Lord." They do not refer to any particular angel.

Some have thought that the angel of the Lord was merely one of a group of special angels who acted in certain instances in the Lord's interest, not necessarily the same angel each time. Others teach that this was an angel, a created angel, but one God had chosen to represent Him in particular situations. Possibly this was a specific, distinct angel authorized by God to such an extent that he was allowed to speak as God.

At times God appeared directly to man. These occasions were recorded in the account of God's dealings with Hagar, Abraham, Jacob, Moses, Joshua, Isaiah, Ezekiel and others. Yet, Scriptures tell us that no one has seen God, and no one can see Him. When Moses asked to see the glory of God, God said to him:

> . . . you cannot see my face, for no one may see me and live. . . . you will see my back; but my face must not be seen [Exodus 33:20, 23b].

In 1 Timothy 1:17 we read that God is invisible, and John tells us that we see God through His Son, Jesus Christ.

> No one has ever seen God, but God the One and Only, who is at the Father's side, has made him known [John 1:18].

When people saw God, it was not actually God they saw, but a form which He allowed them to see.

The Book of John also teaches that only Jesus has seen God. We do not encounter God personally. We are not confronted by God face to face. We learn of Him through His Son. Jesus said,

> No one has seen the Father except the one who is from God; only he has seen the Father [John 6:46].

Then in the Book of 1 John, John tells us that although we don't see Him, God lives in us, and we can see Him through the love we show for each other.

> No one has ever seen God; but if we love one another, God lives in us and his love is made complete in us [1 John 4:12].

Although we know that no one has seen God, in some cases it seems that it was God Himself who appeared as the angel of the Lord. In these references, people who saw this angel often referred to him as God. References which start out discussing the angel of the Lord or the angel of God, later call the same character by God's name.

Was the angel of the Lord the role of Christ before He came to earth as a mortal? Was it the function of Jesus Christ in the Old Testament era, to act in His Father's interest by appearing to men as the angel of the Lord? In order to come to a conclusion as to the identity of this particular angel, we will look at the Scriptures pertaining to the appearances of the angel of the Lord or the angel of God.

HAGAR

The very first time the word *angel* appears in the Bible, it is a reference to the angel of the Lord when he ministered to Hagar in the desert.

> The angel of the Lord found Hagar near a spring in the desert; it was the spring that is beside the road to Shur. And he said, "Hagar, servant of Sarai, where have you come from, and where are you going?"
>
> "I'm running away from my mistress Sarai," she answered.
>
> Then the angel of the Lord told her, "Go back to your mistress and submit to her." The angel added, "I will so increase your descendants that they will be too numerous to count" [Genesis 16:7-10].
>
> She gave this name to the Lord who spoke to her: "You are the God who sees me," for she said, "I have now seen the One who sees me" [Genesis 16:13].

This was not an ordinary, created angel. He promised Hagar He would increase her descendants until they would be "too numerous to count." Hagar knew this angel to be God and said, "You are the God who sees me. . ."

HAGAR/ISHMAEL

After Isaac was born, Sarah begged Abraham to send Hagar and her son away. They wandered in the desert until their water was gone and Ishmael was dying.

God heard the boy crying, and the angel of God called to Hagar from heaven and said to her, "What is the matter, Hagar? Do not be afraid; God has heard the boy crying as he lies there. Lift the boy up and take him by the hand, for I will make him into a great nation."

Then God opened her eyes and she saw a well of water. So she went and filled the skin with water and gave the boy a drink [Genesis 21:17-19].

God heard Ishmael and "the angel of God called to Hagar." Then he stated God's promise to her again.

ABRAHAM

Genesis 22:1 says that "God tested Abraham." When Isaac was older, probably a young man, Abraham was required to demonstrate his faith in a spectacular way. God told Abraham to take Isaac and sacrifice him as a burnt offering. The next morning Abraham left with Isaac and two servants to do as God commanded him. He did not hesitate to sacrifice Isaac because he believed that God could raise him from death (Hebrews 11:19). When Abraham was about to take Isaac's life, he was stopped by the angel of the Lord. God was satisfied with Abraham's response to His command so the angel of the Lord stayed the execution of Isaac.

But the angel of the Lord called out to him from heaven, "Abraham! Abraham!"

"Here I am," he replied.

"Do not lay a hand on the boy," he said. "Do not do anything to him. Now I know that you fear God, because you have not withheld from me your son, your only son" [Genesis 22:11-12].

Abraham found a ram for the sacrifice, and the angel of the Lord spoke from heaven again. This angel who spoke for God repeated God's promise to Abraham.

The angel of the Lord called to Abraham from heaven a second time and said, "I swear by myself, declares the Lord, that because you have done this and have not withheld your son, your only son, I will surely bless you and make your descendants as numerous as the stars in the sky and as the sand on the seashore. Your descendants will take possession of the cities of their enemies, and through your offspring all nations on earth will be blessed, because you have obeyed me" [Genesis 22:15-18].

Notice that the angel of the Lord did not appear to Hagar and Ishmael, or to Abraham and Isaac. In each of these instances the angel called to them from heaven.

JACOB

With the help of his mother Rebekah, Jacob tricked his father Isaac into blessing him instead of his brother Esau. This blessing was significant because it carried with it the inheritance of the firstborn son. Esau resented Jacob's deception and planned to kill him. Rebekah advised Jacob to run away to the home of her brother Laban. Jacob had a dream while he was traveling to Laban's home in Haran to escape his brother's anger.

He had a dream in which he saw a stairway resting on the earth, with its top reaching to heaven, and the angels of God were ascending and decending on it. There above it stood the LORD, and he said: "I am the LORD, the God of your father Abraham and the God of Isaac. I will give you and your descendants the land on which you are lying" [Genesis 28:12-13].

The Lord repeated to Jacob the promise He originally made to Abraham. Jacob was afraid. He said the place was "awesome," and that it was "the house of God," and "the gate of heaven."

Early the next morning Jacob took the stone he had placed under his head and set it up as a pillar and poured oil on top of it. He called that place Bethel. . . [Genesis 28:18-19a].

Jacob was so impressed by this experience that he set up a stone pillar, anointed it, and named the place "Bethel" (house of God). Later we learn the angel of the Lord was "the God of Bethel."

147

Jacob and Laban, his father-in-law, had agreed on a separation of flocks and herds. The streaked, speckled, and spotted animals were to belong to Jacob for his wages. Laban immediately removed all the cattle which had these marks, placed them in the care of his sons, and sent them a distance of three-days-journey.

In spite of Laban's efforts, God caused Jacob to prosper. The means Jacob used to bring about the multiplying of his animals was suggested to him in a dream by the angel of God.

> In breeding season I once had a dream in which I looked up and saw that the male goats mating with the flock were streaked, speckled or spotted. The angel of God said to me in the dream, "Jacob." I answered, "Here I am." And he said, "Look up and see that all the male goats mating with the flock are streaked, speckled or spotted, for I have seen all that Laban has been doing to you. I am the God of Bethel, where you anointed a pillar and where you made a vow to me. Now leave this land at once and go back to your native land" [Genesis 31:10-13].

The angel of God spoke to Jacob saying, "I am the God of Bethel." The one who spoke to him at Bethel said "I am the Lord." The angel of God and God Himself appear to be synonymous.

MOSES

When God called Moses to lead the Israelites out of Egypt, he was a shepherd, working for his father-in-law, Jethro. Moses saw the angel of the Lord in the flames of a bush which burned without being consumed.

> There the angel of the Lord appeared to him in flames of fire from within a bush. Moses saw that though the bush was on fire it did not burn up. So Moses thought, "I will go over and see this strange sight — why the bush does not burn up."
>
> When the Lord saw that he had gone over to look, God called to him from within the bush, "Moses! Moses!"
>
> And Moses said, "Here I am."

"Do not come any closer," God said. "Take off your sandals," for the place where you are standing is holy ground." Then he said, "I am the God of your father, the God of Abraham, the God of Isaac and the God of Jacob." At this, Moses hid his face, because he was afraid to look at God [Exodus 3:2-6].

The angel spoke as God and asked Moses to remove his shoes. This was an act of reverence which would not usually be required by an angel. In Acts, when Stephen spoke of Moses, he said,

This is the same Moses whom they had rejected with the words, "Who made you ruler and judge?" He was sent to be their ruler and deliverer by God himself, through the angel who appeared to him in the bush [Acts 7:35].

We see here that God and the angel are not one and the same because Stephen said that Moses was sent by God through the angel. Although they are almost interchangeable, they are not identical. As we continue this study we shall attempt to determine the identity of the angel of the Lord.

ISRAELITES

On their Exodus from Egypt, the Israelites were accompanied by a pillar of cloud during the day and a pillar of fire at night. These were the visible signs of God's presence with them. At the crossing of the Red Sea the cloud was associated with the angel of God.

Then the angel of God who had been traveling in front of Israel's army, withdrew and went behind them. The pillar of cloud also moved from in front and stood behind them, coming between the armies of Egypt and Israel... [Exodus 14:19-20a].

So the angel of God and the cloud, the symbol of the presence of God, protected Israel by being placed between them and their enemies.

It was the angel of the Lord whom God sent to protect them on their journey. They were warned, by God, not to rebel against this angel. He had the power to forgive sins. If they listened to the angel and did what he said, God would wipe out their enemies. Here, again, we see the subject is the angel and it changes to God.

See, I am sending an angel ahead of you to guard you along the way and to bring you to the place I have prepared. Pay attention to him and listen to what he says. Do not rebel against him; he will not forgive your rebellion, since my Name is in him. If you listen carefully to what he says and do all that I say, I will be an enemy to your enemies and will oppose those who oppose you. My angel will go ahead of you and bring you into the land of the Amorites, Hittites, Perizzites, Canaanites, Hivites and Jebusites, and I will wipe them out [Exodus 23:20-23] (cf. Hebrews 1:4-5).

God said of this angel, "my Name is in him," but we learned from Hebrews 1:4-5 that Christ is superior to the angels because He has the name "Son." Therefore, this was not a created angel.

In the Book of Judges, we learn that this angel who went with the Israelites was the angel of the Lord. He appeared to the Israelites at Bokim to reprimand them for their transgression. The angel of the Lord rebuked the Israelites because they did not remain separate from the people around them. The angel said he brought them out of Egypt and directed them to the land that he promised to give their forefathers. In Genesis 13:14-17, however, it was the Lord who promised the land to Abraham's descendants.

The angel of the Lord went up from Gilgal to Bokim and said, "I brought you up out of Egypt and led you into the land that I swore to give to your forefathers. I said, 'I will never break my covenant with you, and you shall not make a covenant with the people of this land, but you shall break down their altars.' Yet you have disobeyed me. Why have you done this? Now therefore I tell you that I will not drive them out before you; they will be thorns in your sides and their gods will be a snare to you." When the angel of the Lord had spoken these things to all the Israelites, the people wept aloud [Judges 2:1-4].

BALAAM

As the angel of the Lord dealt with the Moabite prophet Balaam, we see another example of the reference transferring the subject from the angel of the Lord, to God.

The angel of the Lord said to Balaam, "Go with the men, but speak only what I tell you." So Balaam went with the princes of Balak [Numbers 22:35].

"Well, I have come to you now," Balaam replied. "But can I say just anything? I must speak only what God puts in my mouth" [Numbers 22:38].

The Lord put a message in Balaam's mouth and said, "Go back to Balak and give him this message" [Numbers 23:5].

The angel of the Lord appeared, first to the donkey, then to Balaam. He said, "speak only what I tell you." It was, however, not the angel but God who gave him the message.

GIDEON

When the angel of the Lord recruited Gideon as a leader, Israel had been oppressed by the Midianites for seven years because they "did evil in the eyes of the Lord." The angel of the Lord called Gideon, but the Lord spoke to him in verses 14 and 16.

When the angel of the Lord appeared to Gideon, he said, "The Lord is with you, mighty warrior" [Judges 6:12].

The Lord turned to him and said, "Go in the strength you have and save Israel out of Midian's hand. Am I not sending you?" [Judges 6:14].

The Lord answered, "I will be with you, and you will strike down all the Midianites together" [Judges 6:16].

When the angel disappeared, Gideon knew that this was the angel of the Lord. Gideon was afraid he would die because he had seen this angel. It was God who spoke to reassure him.

. . .And the angel of the Lord disappeared. When Gideon realized that it was the angel of the Lord, he exclaimed, "Ah Sovereign Lord! I have seen the angel of the Lord face to face!"

But the Lord said to him, "Peace! Do not be afraid. You are not going to die" [Judges 6:21b-23].

MANOAH

This very special angel also appeared to Manoah's wife, and later to Manoah and his wife together. The angel came to tell them they would be the parents of a son and to instruct and guide them concerning his restricted, Nazirite lifestyle. When the angel returned to Manoah's wife, she brought her husband to him. Manoah wanted to prepare food for the angel to eat, but the angel told him to offer a burnt offering to the Lord.

Manoah prepared the sacrifice as the angel instructed. When the angel ascended in the flame, they knew who he was and feared for their lives.

As the flame blazed up from the altar toward heaven, the angel of the Lord ascended in the flame. Seeing this, Manoah and his wife fell with their faces to the ground. When the angel of the Lord did not show himself again to Manoah and his wife, Manoah realized that it was the angel of the Lord.

"We are doomed to die!" he said to his wife. "We have seen God!" [Judges 13:20-22].

Manoah knew that this was the angel of the Lord, but he told his wife, "We have seen God!" Again it seems that the angel of the Lord and God are used as equivalent words or synonyms.

DAVID

David encountered the angel of the Lord when he chose to suffer three days plague as punishment for taking a census of his military forces. As this punishment was happening, God was grieved and stopped the angel (2 Samuel 24:16; 1 Chronicles 21:15). David begged God not to penalize the people for his sin. The angel of the Lord, through the prophet, sent a message to David to build an altar.

David looked up and saw the angel of the Lord, standing between heaven and earth, with a drawn sword in his hand extended over Jerusalem. Then David and the elders, clothed in sackcloth, fell facedown.

David said to God, "Was it not I who ordered the fighting men to be counted? I am the one who has sinned and done wrong. These are but sheep. What have they done? O Lord my God, let your hand fall upon me and my family, but do not let this plague remain on your people."

Then the angel of the Lord ordered Gad to tell David to go up and build an altar to the Lord on the threshing floor of Araunah the Jebusite. So David went up in obedience to the word that Gad had spoken in the name of the Lord [1 Chronicles 21:16-19].

The angel of the Lord gave the message to Gad who was a prophet in David's service, but Gad spoke "in the name of the Lord."

ELIJAH

The angel of the Lord helped Elijah when he was running away from Jezebel. He was afraid because Jezebel had threatened his life. Twice the angel of the Lord provided food for Elijah before he started his long journey to Horeb during which he fasted for forty-days.

Then he lay down under the tree and fell asleep. All at once an angel touched him and said, "Get up and eat." He looked around, and there by his head was a cake of bread baked over hot coals, and a jar of water. He ate and drank and then lay down again.

The angel of the Lord came back a second time and touched him and said, "Get up and eat, for the journey is too much for you." So he got up and ate and drank. Strengthened by that food, he traveled forty days and forty nights until he reached Horeb, the mountain of God [1 Kings 19:5-8].

ELIJAH/KING AHAZIAH

God's judgment on King Ahaziah came through the angel of the Lord to Elijah. Ahaziah was injured and sent messengers to consult a pagan god concerning his recovery. Elijah met the men and gave them the message from the angel of the Lord. This communication condemned the king's idolatry and predicted his death.

But the angel of the Lord said to Elijah the Tishbite, "Go up and meet the messengers of the king of Samaria and ask them, 'Is it because there is no God in Israel that you are going off to consult Baal-Zebub, the god of Ekron?' Therefore this is what the Lord says: 'You will not leave the bed you are lying on. You will certainly die!' " So Elijah went [2 Kings 1:3-4].

When Ahaziah received these words he understood that they had come from Elijah. He sent a captain and fifty men to bring Elijah to him. Elijah, as a prophet of God, was not under the authority of the king. He called fire from heaven to destroy the captain and his men. This was repeated, and a second captain and his fifty men were burned. When the third captain begged Elijah to come to Ahaziah, the angel of the Lord spoke.

The angel of the Lord said to Elijah, "Go down with him; do not be afraid of him." So Elijah got up and went down with him to the king [2 Kings 1:15].

. . ."Because you have done this, you will never leave the bed you are lying on. You will certainly die!" So he died, according to the word of the Lord that Elijah had spoken [2 Kings 1:16b-17].

Elijah repeated the message given to him by the angel of the Lord, and the statement of the angel of the Lord was called "the word of the Lord."

ASSYRIANS

The angel of the Lord came to the aid of Hezekiah when Jerusalem was under attack by Assyria. Sennacherib, King of Assyria, sent his officials to demand that Judah surrender. Hezekiah King of Judah prayed that Jerusalem would be saved from Sennacherib and the Assyrians. Isaiah sent God's answer to Hezekiah.

By the way that he came he will return; he will not enter this city, declares the Lord. I will defend this city and save it, for my sake and for the sake of David my servant."

That night the angel of the Lord went out and put to death a hundred and eighty-five thousand men in the Assyrian camp. When the people got up the next morning — there were all the dead bodies! [2 Kings 19:33-35].

ZECHARIAH

Zechariah was a prophet during the time following the Exile. In one night Zechariah received eight visions which were symbolic messages of prophecy sent to him from God. The angel of the Lord, in this instance, spoke to God for man. God's answer was communicated by the interpreting angel who was explaining the visions to Zechariah.

Then the angel of the Lord said, "Lord Almighty, how long will you withhold mercy from Jerusalem and from the towns of Judah, which you have been angry with these seventy years?" So the Lord spoke kind and comforting words to the angel who talked with me.

Then the angel who was speaking to me said, "Proclaim this word: This is what the Lord Almighty says: 'I am very jealous for Jerusalem and Zion' " [Zechariah 1:12-14].

MALACHI

Malachi tells us of two messengers. The first of these was John the Baptist who prepared the way, or was the forerunner. The second, the messenger of the Covenant, was Jesus, the Messiah. He was the communicator between God and man.

"See, I will send my messenger, who will prepare the way before me. Then suddenly the Lord you are seeking will come to his temple; the messenger of the covenant, whom you desire, will come," says the Lord Almighty [Malachi 3:1].

The New Testament records Jesus' teaching that He was the messenger of His Father, speaking what the Father commanded.

For I did not speak of my own accord, but the Father who sent me commanded me what to say and how to say it. I know that his command leads to eternal life. So whatever I say is just what the Father has told me to say [John 12:49-50].

REFERENCES INTENTIONALLY OMITTED

There are two scriptural accounts which are usually included in a study of the angel of the Lord. In a sincere effort to make no assumption which the Scripture does not support, we are excluding the visit to Abraham, and the man who appeared to Joshua from our study of the angel of the Lord. The occasion when three men visited Abraham is recorded in Genesis 18:1 - 19:13. Three men appeared to Abraham but only two angels went to Sodom. Some would conclude that the other was the angel of the Lord, because he dealt with Abraham as only God could. This passage of Scripture, however, does not mention the angel of the Lord.

There is also a biblical character who appeared to Joshua before the fall of Jericho, whom some would call the angel of the Lord. This account is found in Joshua 5:13 - 6:2. A messenger came to Joshua with a drawn sword. He identified himself as "a commander of the Lord's army." He asked Joshua to remove his sandals because he was standing on a holy place. It was the angel of the Lord who asked Moses to perform this same act of reverence. This account does not make reference directly or indirectly to the angel of the Lord. Therefore, it will not be included in this section.

We have seen from these examples that the angel of the Lord is Himself the Lord, and yet He is distinguished from the Father. In a way which we cannot fully comprehend, there are three members of the Godhead, or the

Trinity. The Scripture presents God as the one and only God, but He is also proclaimed to us as the Father, the Son, and the Holy Spirit, three separate distinct personal identities.

So, who was the angel of the Lord? In answer to this question, Guy N. Woods said, ". . .it is beyond reasonable doubt a reference to the second person of the Godhead — Jesus Christ our Lord" (*Gospel Advocate*/July 1988).

In the article "The Angel of Jehovah," John Waddey said, "These many references demonstrate that our Lord existed from eternity with the Father, . . . They tell us of the Savior's activities in behalf of the redeemed during those long years when mankind groped in darkness for a guiding hand, before He came as Jesus, the son of Mary (*Sound Doctrine*/January 1982).

SUMMARY

The angel of the Lord acted as no other angel did. He referred to Himself as God, and God said, "my Name is in him" [Exodus 23:21]. He not only spoke for God, He spoke as God. He required Moses to show reverence by removing his shoes. He had the power to forgive sins.

The angel of the Lord is the Lord Himself, and yet He is also separate and distinct from God the Father. Jehovah is the one and the only God who is revealed to us through Scripture as the Father, His Son, and His Spirit. All are one, yet each one is distinct. There is much evidence to say that the role of the angel of the Lord was one of the functions of the Son of God.

REVIEW

1. Give several possible explanations of the identity of the angel of the Lord._____

_____

2. What is unusual about this angel? _____

_____

3. Who has seen God? _____

_____

4. In Scripture regarding the angel of the Lord, how does the subject of the sentence change within the passage?_____

5. How many people, or groups of people, can you name who were linked with the angel of the Lord?____

6. What, in your opinion, is the identity of the angel of the Lord?_____

NOTES

_____
_____
_____
_____
_____
_____
_____
_____
_____
_____
_____
_____
_____
_____
_____
_____
_____
_____
_____
_____
_____
_____

Chapter Eleven

The Death Angel?

DEATH ANGEL CONCEPT

There are several theories prevalent today concerning an angel who has been given the name **death angel**. What does the term **death angel** mean to you? When you read or hear this term are you caused to think of the occasion when the eldest son, in every family of the Egyptian nation, died in one night?

Or, does this phrase make you imagine an angel who appears to a person who is dying? Do you think, as the ancient Jews did, that he will come to separate your soul and body at the moment of physical death?

There is also a third possibility for the name of **death angel**. Although Scripture does not call him this, any angel who was sent by God on a mission to destroy human life, may be called a **death angel**.

The visual image of the death angel is quite different from the "treetop angel" which we described at the beginning of our investigation. Hopefully, we erased that concept by a study of the Scripture.

Let's consider now the possibility that the death angel was an angel who came to bring the final plague to the Egyptians. Although this was the tenth plague to be inflicted on them, it was the first one that God described to Moses.

"Then say to Pharaoh, 'This is what the Lord says: Israel is my firstborn son, and I told you, "Let my son go, so he may worship me. But you refused to let him go; so I will kill your firstborn son' " [Exodus 4:22-23].

Some of us have a picture in our minds, probably from childhood, of the death angel as a shadowy figure who hovered over the doorway of each house looking for blood on the framework. Finding the symbolic stain, he quickly passed over the dwelling, but if he did not find the blood, he took the life of the firstborn son and the firstborn of all the cattle as well. This is the act which was commemorated annually by the Jews in the Feast of the Passover.

FEAST OF THE PASSOVER

The Feast of the Passover was a festival observed by the Jews to recollect the meal eaten in haste before the escape from Egypt. It was one of three rituals which all devout Jews celebrated by coming to Jerusalem to worship at the temple. The Passover was instituted by God to commemorate the Exodus from Egypt. The observance lasted seven days, and in Exodus 23:15 it is called "the Feast of Unleavened Bread."

The Passover meal consisted of unleavened bread, bitter herbs, and roasted lamb. Each of these items had a particular meaning to the Israelites. The blood of the lamb marked their residences and distinguished their homes from those of the Egyptians.

> This is a day you are to commemorate; for the generations to come you shall celebrate it as a festival to the LORD—a lasting ordinance. For seven days you are to eat bread made without yeast. On the first day remove the yeast from your houses, for whoever eats anything with yeast in it from the first day through the seventh must be cut off from Israel. On the first day hold a sacred assembly, and another one on the seventh day, Do no work at all on these days, except to prepare food for everyone to eat—that is all you may do.

Celebrate the Feast of Unleavened Bread, because it was on this very day that I brought your divisions out of Egypt. Celebrate this day for a lasting ordinance for the generations to come [Exodus 12:14-17].

160

DEATH ANGEL IN EXODUS?

It may be surprising to you to learn that the Death Angel is not revealed in chapters 11 and 12 of The Book of Exodus, which is the record of the plague of the firstborn and the institution of the Passover. In fact, there is no mention of any angel in either of these chapters. And what is more surprising, the phrase "death angel," does not appear in the entire Bible.

DESTRUCTIVE ANGELS OF THE OLD TESTAMENT

The Old Testament records occasions when an angel was sent by God to annihilate those who were sinful. We have considered some of these events already in our investigation. God provided an angel to eliminate the Canaanite nations who were the enemies of the Israelites.

> I will send an angel before you and drive out the Canaanites, Amorites, Hittites, Perizzites, Hivites and Jebusites [Exodus 33:2].

Although there was no mention of an angel in the Egyptian plague, notice that this reference connects an angel with another plague. The angel of the Lord brought on Jerusalem a three-day-plague to punish David's sin of counting his military troops.

> So the LORD sent a plague on Israel from that morning until the end of the time designated, and seventy thousand of the people from Dan to Beersheba died. When the angel stretched out his hand to destroy Jerusalem, the LORD was grieved because of the calamity and said to the angel who was afflicting the people, "Enough! Withdraw your hand." The angel of the LORD was then at the threshing floor of Araunah the Jebusite [2 Samuel 24:15-16].

Some commentaries tell us the angel or messenger was only a suffocating wind, a disease, or pestilence, but David and Araunah and his sons saw the angel and were frightened.

While Araunah was threshing wheat, he turned and saw the angel; his four sons who were with him hid themselves [1 Chronicles 21:20].

It was the angel of the Lord who rescued Hezekiah and Jerusalem from King Sennacherib, and the Assyrian army was the victim of this destructive angel.

That night the angel of the LORD went out and put to death a hundred and eighty-five thousand men in the Assyrian camp. When the people got up the next morning—there were all the dead bodies! [2 Kings 19:35].

David the Psalmist requested that God deal with those who attacked him as if they were being forced out and chased by the angel of the Lord. We see that even the poetry of the Psalms described the angel of the Lord as destructive.

May they be like chaff before the wind, with the angel of the LORD driving them away; may their path be dark and slippery with the angel of the LORD pursuing them [Psalm 35:5-6].

If we must award the name "death angel," these angels from the Old Testament are certainly well qualified to receive the title.

DESTRUCTIVE ANGELS IN THE NEW TESTAMENT

The New Testament also represented angels as forces of destruction. Jesus told His disciples the meaning of the parable of the weeds. He said the weeds were the children of the devil and the reapers were the angels who will burn the weeds.

As the weeds are pulled up and burned in the fire, so it will be at the end of the age. The Son of Man will send out his angels, and they will weed out of his kingdom everything that causes sin and all who do evil [Matthew 13:40-41].

An angel of the Lord took the life of Herod Agrippa I. He was the king who had James the son of Zebedee beheaded, and Peter put into prison. He allowed the people to flatter him with claims that he was a god. Because he did not refuse this praise, and direct it to God instead, an angel took his life. Josephus tells us that he died in five days.

> On the appointed day Herod, wearing his royal robes, sat on his throne and delivered a public address to the people. They shouted, "This is the voice of a god, not of a man." Immediately, because Herod did not give praise to God, an angel of the Lord struck him down, and he was eaten by worms and died [Acts 12:21-23].

The angel who struck Herod and the ones who will weed out the kingdom also have a right to claim the name "death angel."

"THE DESTROYER"

We are certain that at times God used angels as messengers of destruction and death. Was this the case with the tenth plague? Does the Scripture say the final plague against Pharaoh was brought about through the agency of angels?

Moses spoke to the elders of Israel and told them that the Lord would go through the land and strike down the Egyptians, and when He saw the blood on their doorframes, He would pass over them.

> When the LORD goes through the land to strike down the Egyptians, he will see the blood on the top and sides of the doorframe and will pass over that doorway, and he will not permit the destroyer to enter your houses and strike you down [Exodus 12:23].

God would not allow "the destroyer" to go into the houses of the Israelites nor harm them. "The destroyer" was whatever means God used to accomplish the destruction of the Egyptian firstborn.

The writer of the Book of Hebrews referred to "the destroyer" when he spoke of Moses keeping the Passover.

> By faith he kept the Passover and the sprinkling
> of blood, so that the destroyer of the firstborn would
> not touch the firstborn of Israel [Hebrews 11:28].

Although there was no allusion to an angel in this passage, tradition has taken the term "the destroyer" and created an accompanying legend which has become almost universally accepted.

The Bible says that the Lord passed over the blood-stained homes and they were unharmed. The dwellings of the Egyptians were not marked with blood, thus the Lord took the life of their firstborn sons and their animals. The Bible is not specific in relation to the method God used to affect this blow to the Egyptian people. Does this mean we are free to speculate and theorize concerning His procedure? Because angels are God's messengers and sometimes brought about destruction, shall we suppose that they were His representatives in this action?

Look at the Scriptures which refer to this deed and see whether they justify the fantasy of the "Death Angel."

> So I will stretch out my hand and strike the
> Egyptians with all the wonders that I will perform
> among them. After that, he will let you go [Exodus
> 3:20].

> So Moses said, "This is what the LORD says: 'About
> midnight I will go throughout Egypt. Every firstborn
> son in Egypt will die, from the firstborn son of
> Pharaoh, who sits on the throne, to the firstborn son
> of the slave girl, who is at her hand mill, and all the
> firstborn of the cattle as well. There will be loud
> wailing throughout Egypt — worse than there has ever
> been or ever will be again. But among the Israelites
> not a dog will bark at man or animal.' Then you will
> know that the LORD makes a distinction between
> Egypt and Israel. All these officials of yours will come
> to me, bowing down before me and saying, 'Go, you
> and all the people who follow you!' After that I will
> leave." Then Moses, hot with anger, left Pharaoh
> [Exodus 11:4-8].

On that same night I will pass through Egypt and strike down every firstborn—both men and animals—and I will bring judgment on all the gods of Egypt. I am the LORD. The blood will be a sign for you on the houses where you are; and when I see the blood, I will pass over you. No destructive plague will touch you when I strike Egypt [Exodus 12:12-13].

We may see a connection between "the destructive plague" and "the destroyer" as we continue to study. We find that Paul also mentioned "the destroyer" in writing to the Corinthians. He warned:

And do not grumble, as some of them did—and were killed by the destroying angel [1 Corinthians 10:10].

The term *destroying angel* would be more correctly translated *destroyer* as the King James and American Standard Versions have translated the Greek word *olothreutes*.

There is another Greek word in the Book of Revelation which referred to an angel and had the meaning *destroyer.*

They had as king over them the angel of the Abyss, whose name in Hebrew is Abaddon, and in Greek, Apollyon [Revelation 9:11].

Both the name "Abaddon" and "Apolloyon," mean *destroyer.* The Greek word is *apollumi.* When used as a proper noun it is *apolluon.* Therefore the *destroyer* of 1 Corinthians 10:10 was not the "angel of the abyss" (Vine 302-3).

The "grumbling" was a reference to Numbers 16. It was more than grumbling or complaining as we think of it. They falsely accused Moses and Aaron for something that the Lord had done.

The next day the whole Israelite community grumbled against Moses and Aaron. "You have killed the LORD'S people," they said [Numbers 16:41].

A study of Numbers 16:42-49 does not reveal the participation of an angel in this plague.

We saw plague associated with an angel of devastation in 2 Samuel 24:15-16. We know, however, that "three days of plague" was one of the choices of punishment offered to David by the prophet Gad. Since this plague was dispensed by an angel, shall we assume that all plagues were administered by angels?

In 1 Corinthians chapter ten, Paul warned the people with examples from Israel's history. Verse ten used the word "destroyer" to refer to the plague which was recorded in Numbers 16. Some people equate "the destroyer" with the angel of death or the "destroying angel," but, not all plagues were enforced by angels. Consider verse eight, which referred to a plague in Numbers 25. It did not say an angel was involved, but merely stated ". . .and in one day 23,000 of them died" [1 Corinthians 10:8].

Commenting on 1 Corinthians 10:10, Adam Clarke says,

> The Jews suppose that God employed destroying angels to punish those rebellious Israelites: they were five in number, and one of them they call the destroyer *(Bethany Parallel Commentary on the New Testament)*.

The New International Version Study Bible footnote explains 1 Corinthians 10:10 as follows:

> Paul links the angel who brought the plague of Numbers 16:46-50 — because of the grumbling of the Israelites against Moses and Aaron (Numbers 16:41) — with the destroying angel of Exodus 12:23.

In two out of every three Old Testament histories, commentaries, and reference books which were consulted, the angel of death was said to have carried out the final plague against Egypt. There is very little questioning which takes place in our minds when we consult such reference books. We usually read them, accept them, and go on, informed or misinformed. It should become our habit to question the information we accept as truth.

"BAND OF DESTROYING ANGELS"

There is a verse in the Book of Psalms which must be included in our study. The writer gave warning not to repeat Israel's mistakes. He pointed out that the plagues were in preparation for Israel's deliverance. In doing this, he briefly outlined the plagues. Only the first and last are in sequence, and three are omitted entirely. He referred to the final plague as the work of "a band of destroying angels" ("evil angels" KJV).

> He unleashed against them his hot anger, his wrath, indignation and hostility—a band of destroying angels. He prepared a path for his anger; he did not spare them from death but gave them over to the plague. He struck down all the firstborn of Egypt, the firstfruits of manhood in the tents of Ham [Psalm 78:49-51].

Notice this is not a reference to *the death angel*, but "a band of destroying angels." In the poetic language of the Psalms, this may not be a literal reference to spirit beings.

The footnote on Psalm 78:49, the NIV Study Bible indicates,

> The poet personifies God's wrath, indignation, and hostility as agents of his anger.

It is perhaps an indication on the part of the Psalmist, of an unwillingness to attribute to the Lord, such an act as the destruction of the firstborn. Therefore, he pictured God's exasperation, as the work of a band of evil angels.

On this verse, Adam Clarke observed,

> This is the first mention we have of *evil angels*. There is no mention of them in the account we have of the plagues of Egypt in the Book of Exodus, and what they were we cannot tell. An angel or "messenger" may be either animate or inanimate, a disembodied spirit or human being, any thing or being that is an instrument sent of God for the punishment or support of mankind.

To summarize the information, consider these points: (1) God said He would kill the firstborn son of the Egyptians. (2) God sent angels on destructive missions in both Old and New Testament times. (3) Exodus 12:23 called the force which killed the Egyptian sons "the destroyer." (4) Paul wrote to warn the Corinthians, saying the

Israelites were killed by "the destroyer," when they complained. (5) The writer of Hebrews used this same term, "the destroyer," to refer to the prevention of injury to the sons of Israel by the sprinkling of blood. (6) The Psalmist used the phrase "a band of destroying angels," to describe the anger of God against the Egyptians.

DEATH ANGEL ACCOMPANIES FAITHFUL TO PARADISE?

If we define the death angel as an angel who escorted the faithful to paradise, we must consider the story of the rich man and Lazarus. Luke told of "the angels," not the death angel, carrying Lazarus to be with Abraham in paradise. The example was one of angels escorting the dead, not one of the death angel.

> The time came when the beggar died and the angels carried him to Abraham's side. The rich man also died and was buried [Luke 16:22].

DEATH

From the time that Eve first yielded to the temptation of the serpent in the Garden, human beings came under the penalty of sin which is death.

Job was cynical when he spoke to God of the uncertainty of life, of man's heritage as trouble, and his fate as death.

> Man born of woman is of few days and full of trouble. He springs up like a flower and withers away; like a fleeting shadow, he does not endure [Job 14:1-2].

Death was always surrounded in mystery because of the fear of the unknown, therefore, people created legends and fables to explain that which they did not understand. The literature and folklore of many nations included legends of the Death Angel.

DEATH ANGEL/JEWISH FOLKLORE

Jewish folktales retold the stories recorded in the Old Testament. The following paragraph is taken from a book written for children, *The Tale of Ancient Israel*. It contains Old Testament stories retold by Roger Lancelyn Green.

At midnight the Messenger of Jahveh, Azrael the Angel of Death, passed over the land of Egypt and slew the first-born of all who dwelt there, from the eldest son of Pharaoh to the eldest child of the captive in his dungeon, and the first-born of the cattle also. But over every house marked with three splashes of blood Azrael passed without touching any of the inmates with his sword — and not one of the Israelites nor of their cattle died that night.

In Jewish folklore the Angel of Death was symbolized by an angel who stood between heaven and earth, holding a sword which dripped with poison. The Angel of Death was supposed to remove the soul from the body of the dying person.

The Jews gave the Death Angel the name Azrael, and he was assisted by another angel named Sammael. Sammael's responsibility was to gather the souls of Jews who died outside Israel, but it was thought highly improbable that the soul of the Jew who died a wanderer would ever reach paradise.

Sammael was associated with the "king of terrors" in Job 18:14. Bildad was discussing with Job the destiny of the righteous and the wicked. He maintained the wicked received punishment in this life, while Job asserted that the sinful succeeded and the upright were afflicted. The "king of terrors" was clearly a reference to death.

It eats away parts of his skin; death's firstborn devours his limbs. He is torn from the security of his tent and marched off to the king of terrors [Job 18:13-14].

The mythology of Canaan told of a god of death and sterility whose name was Mot. The perpetual recurrence of death was one of his responsibilities. Mot was the god of the dead and of the forces which opposed life and fertility. In Canaanite literature he was portrayed as a god who swallowed up his victim.

Many traditions of the Jews were related to their acceptance of the Angel of Death in ancient times, especially those related to death, burial, and mourning. It was believed that this angel, though unseen, was the cause of the misfortune of death. Customs such as closing the eyes of the dead, go back to folklore concerning the Angel of Death. Legend said that when the Angel of Death took a life, he then washed his sword in water. From this came the superstition that all water must be poured out, in the house where death has occurred.

The Encyclopaedia Judaica related a tale of Jewish belief and the Death Angel. The reason the dead body gave off a bad odor was the work of the Death Angel. The dying person saw the Death Angel standing over him and opened his mouth in fright. When he did the angel dropped one drop of gall into the dying mouth from the tip of his sword. The swallowing of this drop of gall at the instant of death caused the corpse to have an offensive smell.

This story is also from *The Encyclopaedia Judaica*. If a dying person were in great pain, it would not be desirable for the person to linger. It was their belief that holy objects deterred the Death Angel in his work of taking life. Therefore, the *mezuzah* was taken from the door and sacred books were removed from the room, because their nearness would weaken the power of the Death Angel.

At weddings it was common for skits to be performed in which the Death Angel, portrayed as an old man with white hair, was overcome by a young girl. We think this was related to a verse in the Book of Jeremiah.

> Then maidens will dance and be glad, young men and old as well. I will turn their mourning into gladness. . . [Jeremiah 31:13a].

Other productions presented the Angel of Death as a married man with a family. He was usually assisted, but occasionally harassed, by his wife. She helped him by killing babies and harming pregnant women and women in childbirth. In these stories, the theme was man's revenge on the angel, illustrated by satire.

The custom of wearing black clothing to symbolize mourning was not accepted among Jewish people. In ancient times the Near Eastern people traditionally wore white but dressed in dark colors to hide from the Death Angel. Although the Jews taught and believed in the

Death Angel, they rejected the pagan practice of wearing black to symbolize grief.

The Jews believed that the Angel of Death was one of the "fallen angels." Commenting on the phrase, "him who has the power of death," which is from Hebrews 2:14, Adam Clarke said,

> This is spoken in conformity to an opinion prevalent among the Jews that there was a certain fallen angel who was called the "angel of death."

The legends of ancient times show that the storyteller had a great influence on the people. For centuries, these tales were repeated orally generation after generation. Now they are collected and recorded for our information and entertainment. The next story is paraphrased from such a source.

Sammael, the Angel of Death was sent to end the life of Abraham. The Lord told him to put aside his terrible appearance and take the form of a charming, radiant angel. In the form of a good-looking young man, he went to Abraham to take his soul "with all gentleness."

Abraham asked Sammael who he was, where he came from, and where he was going. So Sammael told Abraham who he was and why he had come. Abraham asked if he always appeared in this beautiful form and was told that to sinners he appeared in a horrible form. "But to the just I appear with a crown of light upon my head, like a divine messenger of peace."

Abraham wanted to see him in his terrible form. So Sammael "appeared with seven dragon heads and fourteen faces." The sight must have been horrible because the story says that seven thousand of the household servants died and Abraham fainted from the sight. When Abraham regained consciousness he prayed for his servants to be restored and the angel, Michael, brought them back to life. Sammael resumed the shape of a beautiful angel, but Abraham refused to give up his soul.

Finally God commanded Michael to entice away his soul as if he were dreaming. So the angels came from heaven and took Abraham's soul and placed it in "heaven-spun garments like snow, and bore it away on a fiery chariot"

171

[Angel S. Rappoport, Ph.D., *Ancient Israel, Myths and Legends*].

ANGEL OF DEATH/ISLAMIC BELIEF

In Mohammedan belief, the Arabs who worship Allah believe in an Angel of Death named Azrael. Their sacred book, the Koran, teaches that he had many assistants who were assigned to separate the souls from the bodies of the dead. Their duties depend on whether the person has lived a righteous or a wicked life. If the person has been upright, the soul is taken very tenderly, but an evil person's soul was violently ripped from him.

> Those who return to unbelief after Allah's guidance has been revealed to them are seduced by Satan and inspired by him. That is because they say to those who abhor the word of Allah; "We shall obey you in some matters." Allah knows their secret talk.

> What will they do when the angels carry away their souls and strike them on their heads and backs?

> That is because they follow what has incurred the wrath of Allah and abhor what pleases him. He will surely bring their works to nothing [Koran 47:25-28].

> Say: "The angel of death, who has been given charge of you, will carry off your souls. Then to your Lord you shall all return" [Koran 32:11].

ANGEL OF DEATH/MYTHOLOGY

There was a theory in mythology associated with a belief in the Angel of Death. This was the belief that the soul was accompanied to its home in the afterlife by a messenger. In Greek mythology, the personality was Hermes, and in Roman belief, it was the God, Mercury. In addition to being the messenger of the gods, one of the duties of Hermes or Mercury was to guide the dead to Hades.

Pluto was the God of the underworld and Hades was his home. The River Styx flowed throughout Hades and must be crossed to reach the afterlife. This required the services of the boatman, Charon. He ferried the souls over the River Styx to reach Hades.

SUMMARY

A study of the Scripture does not specifically indictate that a particular angel, the "death angel," acted to take the lives of the eldest son in each family of the nation of Egypt. We do find instances when angels were destructive to those who provoked God's anger.

Neither is there scriptural evidence to support the theory that an angel, the "Death Angel," was designated to bring an end to physical life. Luke gave example of angels conducting the dead to paradise, but no death angel. The Death Angel is found in many stories which have survived from ancient Jewish folklore. Islamic doctrine also teaches belief in an Angel of Death. There was a Death Angel in Greek and Roman mythology. We find that these angels and their participation in the death process is purely superstition.

REVIEW

1. Describe your concept of the death angel before this study. _____

_____

2. What was the Feast of the Passover?_____

_____

3. How were the firstborn sons of Egypt killed?_____

_____

4. Give some scriptural examples of destructive angels.

_____

_____

5. What was the meaning of "the destroyer" in Exodus 12:23 and Hebrews 11:28? _____

_____

6. Who does Paul use as an example in his warning 1 Corinthians 10:10?_____

_____

7. Was an angel associated with the plague which is recorded in Numbers 16?_____

8. What was the meaning of "a band of destroying angels" in Psalm 78:49?_____

9. How was the Angel of Death depicted by Jewish folklore?_____

10. What did Mohammed teach concerning the Death Angel? _____

NOTES

_____
_____
_____
_____
_____
_____
_____
_____
_____
_____
_____
_____
_____
_____
_____
_____
_____
_____
_____
_____
_____
_____
_____
_____

Chapter Twelve

My Guardian Angel?

D o you have a guardian angel? Do I? Does everyone? Does anyone? What is a guardian angel? In this study we shall question who is eligible to receive the ministry of a guardian angel. We shall consider the purpose and possible duties of the guardian angel. Then we want to learn what the Scripture teaches on the subject and finally we shall question what other sources of information may have influenced our beliefs.

The whole sentiment of the guardian angel is a very comforting view. It gives us a secure feeling to imagine an individual angel who is on guard, around-the-clock, for our advantage. Still, there is a problem with the belief. The question is, who is at fault when something unfortunate happens to me? Did my angel fail me? Think of the person who, as we say, "has more than her share of troubles." Was this individual assigned a faulty angel or has the angel just been negligent?

GOD'S ANGELS PROTECTED PEOPLE

We have many examples of God's people being protected, rescued, and reassured by angels. In these examples, you will notice the angel was God's angel and was not designated as Daniel's angel, the apostles' angel, Peter's angel, or Paul's angel.

Daniel:
My God sent his angel, and he shut the mouths of the lions. They have not hurt me, because I was

found innocent in his sight. Nor have I ever done any wrong before you, O king [Daniel 6:22].

Apostles:

But during the night an angel of the Lord opened the doors of the jail and brought them out [Acts 5:19].

Peter:

Then Peter came to himself and said, "Now I know without a doubt that the Lord sent his angel and rescued me from Herod's clutches and from everything the Jewish people were anticipating" [Acts 12:11].

Paul:

Last night an angel of the God whose I am and whom I serve stood beside me and said, "Do not be afraid, Paul. You must stand trial before Caesar, and God has graciously given you the lives of all who sail with you" [Acts 27:23-24].

GUARDIAN ANGEL CONCEPT

Who is eligible to receive the aid or service of a guardian angel? What are the requirements? Some people say that every soul has a guardian angel assigned to it at birth. Others claim this is a benefit which is reserved for believers, only as long as they remain faithful. Jews, Christians, and pagans as well, shared the belief that angels were sent to care for and defend them.

The purpose of the guardian angel is to protect the person from harm, injury, or danger. He is also presumed to guide him or her in safe paths both physically and spiritually. The guardian angel is a source of strength when one is provoked to anger or tempted by worldly attractions.

There is another theory that this angel functions in a role somewhat like that of a conscience and guides one away from wrong choices and evil influences. Some people have an idea that their guardian angel is a miniature, complete with wings and halo, sitting on the shoulder and persuading one to do right. This may even be enlarged to include the opposite extent. That is an evil angel with horns and a pitchfork who urges one to be dishonest or sinful.

SCRIPTURAL TEACHING

Even though the Scriptures do not use the term "guardian angel," some references are considered vaguely applicable. There are several passages that come to mind when we discuss the possibility of guardian angels, but we shall always have difficulty when we take a theoretical notion, not specified in Scripture, and attempt to find a biblical text to justify it.

PSALM 34:7

When we seek to defend the guardian angel argument this verse from Psalms is usually the one we quote first.

The angel of the LORD encamps around those who fear him, and he delivers them [Psalm 34:7].

This angel was the angel of the covenant and the covenant was made by God with Israel. This verse teaches that God provided protection for His people, as a nation, and as individuals. It does not teach that He assigned an angel to each one of them or to each of us.

PSALM 91:11-12

Another beautiful promise concerning the ministering of angels is found in the Book of Psalms.

For he will command his angels concerning you to guard you in all your ways; they will lift you up in their hands, so that you will not strike your foot against a stone [Psalm 91:11-12].

God used angels for the protection of His people. This description of tender care suggested the concern of a nursemaid for a small child. The devil used this text in his temptation of Jesus. It appeared in Matthew 4:6 and Luke 4:10-11. Satan omitted the clause, "to guard you in all your ways," which did not suit his purpose. Even though this beautiful language suggested a comfortable security, it was not the promise of a guardian angel.

DANIEL 4:13

Some would say that Daniel 4:13 referred to guardian angels. The King James Version says, "a watcher and an holy one."

> In the visions I saw while lying in my bed, I looked, and there before me was a messenger, a holy one, coming down from heaven [Daniel 4:13].

This angel was called a "watcher" because of his watching or observing in expectation of carrying out God's will.

MATTHEW 18:10

When we go to the New Testament we also find some references which many individuals cite to substantiate the questionable doctrine of guardian angels. The standard concept of the guardian angel today, that is an angel assigned to protect little children, probably comes from this verse.

> See that you do not look down on one of these little ones. For I tell you that their angels in heaven always see the face of my Father in heaven [Matthew 18:10].

Read the verse in the context of the eighteenth chapter, beginning with verse one. Jesus called a child to Him and told His disciples to become *like* this child in order to enter the kingdom of heaven; to be humble like a child in order to be the greatest; and to welcome little children in His name. But in verse six it changed to "little ones who believe in me," which was not a reference to children but to His disciples.

The significant term in this verse is "their angels." The pronoun "their" referred to the followers of Jesus, not to little children. The emphasis of the verse was a caution to any who would "look down on" or "despise" (KJV) these believers. The verse spoke of "their angels" in the nature of a warning.

The description of angels always seeing the face of the Father was an example of the earthly ruler who allowed those with the most influence to be in the closest proximity to the throne. The reference was a warning that the disciples had God's protection, during that miraculous age, through particular angels. It did not assure a guardian angel for each person then or now.

ACTS 12:13-15

Herod put Peter in prison, waiting until after the Passover to bring him to trial. An angel came to the prison while Peter was asleep, chained between two soldiers and guarded by sentries. The angel escorted Peter past the guards, out into the street, and left him. At first Peter did not realize the angel had rescued him from Herod, but thought he was dreaming. He went to the home of Mary, where the church was praying to God for him.

> Peter knocked at the outer entrance, and a servant girl named Rhoda came to answer the door. When she recognized Peter's voice, she was so overjoyed she ran back without opening it and exclaimed, "Peter is at the door!"
> "You're out of your mind," they told her. When she kept insisting that it was so, they said, "It must be his angel" [Acts 12:13-15].

Many people think this was a reference to Peter's guardian angel. On the contrary, it would seem to be anything but his guardian angel. If those who were gathered at Mary's house believed Peter were still alive, what would his guardian angel be doing there? It is more likely that they believed Herod had killed Peter and this was Peter's ghost or his spirit. Notice that Rhoda did not see Peter, she only heard his voice.

It is probably true that the overstated doctrine of angels taught by the Jews had entered the knowledge of these people. In reference to this text, Adam Clarke said,

> It was a common opinion among the Jews that every man has a guardian angel, . . .

The question for us is not whether the Jews believed it, but whether it is substantiated by Scripture.

Clarke continued:

> As *angelos* signifies in general "a messenger," whether divine or human, some have thought that the angel

179

here means a servant or person which the disciples supposed was sent from Peter to announce something of importance to the brethren.

It is not likely, however, that these people would identify Peter's voice with a messenger sent by him. Nor would they insist that Rhoda was insane because Peter sent them a message.

HEBREWS 1:14

The writer of the Book of Hebrews often spoke of angels, especially in the first and second chapters. One of the meaningful things he told us was that angels were sent to attend the ones who would be saved.

Are not all angels ministering spirits sent to serve those who will inherit salvation? [Hebrews 1:14].

This verse used a figure of speech which was written in the interrogative mode. It did not indicate that the writer was expressing a doubt, but that he was placing positive emphasis on a fact. This fact, however, was stated, or written to the Hebrews in a time when the miraculous or supernatural age was still in effect. There is absolutely no similarity in the ministering of God's spirit messengers and the assumption that every faithful Christian is protected by a personal angel.

The Scriptures cannot be used to prove that individuals have guardian angels. There is not an example of a designated angel appointed to precisely guard or influence a particular person. The Bible is not specific and it cannot be cited as an illustration of the appointment of a guardian angel, the eligibility of one to receive the services of a guardian angel, or what the work of a guardian angel may be.

OTHER SOURCES

Outside the pages of Scripture there is a wealth of information about the guardian angel. It ranges in derivation from the comic section of the newspaper to classical literature. There are guardian angel themes in television's situation comedies and award-winning dramas.

They are contained in the front page stories of the tabloid newspapers and in the lyrics of popular love songs.

BABYLONIAN PRACTICE

Charles F. Pfeiffer, writing in *Old Testament History*, said that the Babylonian polytheistic belief included a personal god whom they thought was their defender and supplier. This form of a "guardian angel" never left the person unless he committed a dreadful sin.

In the countries which were neighbors to the Israelites in ancient times, people needed a being who was closer than the gods, an obliging guardian who would help the ordinary people and intercede for them with the gods. The idea became assimilated into Jewish teachings. To maintain their monotheistic belief, the guardians became angels instead of minor gods.

PERSIAN BELIEF

Zoroastrianism is the smallest living religion in the world today. It was the pre-Islamic religion of Persia which is now Iran. The captivity of the Jews by Babylon occurred shortly before the end of Zoroaster's life. He was a Persian prophet of the 6th century B.C. He had an influence on King Cyrus who later ruled the exiled Jews after conquering Babylon. Cyrus was responsible for the Jews return to Judah, but they remained subjects of Zoroastrian kings for two hundred years. Zoroaster taught a belief in throngs of guardian angels and he said men are guided by the spirit of truth and hindered by the spirit of evil.

POST-EXILIC JUDAISM

A belief in the guardian angel became important in the teachings of Judaism after the Exile. This resulted from their orientation into the Persian religion and its angelology. It was not unusual for the Jews in the first century to believe in a guardian angel for each person.

TRADITIONAL JEWISH TRAINING

Jewish children were taught that an angel accompanied them to the synagogue on the Sabbath. If the child had been good, the angel was pleased. They were, however, expected to accept this teaching as legend — not doctrine.

There was another Jewish story, which said that a good angel and an evil angel always accompanied man. They especially were with him on the eve of the Sabbath. As he was returning from the synagogue, for every command that he obeyed, God sent him a protecting angel.

MYTHOLOGICAL PRECEPT

A *genius*, in Roman mythology, was a spirit or creative force which occupied a human being. The birth of the genii occurred at the same time as that of their mortals and they remained together until life ended. It was their role to shape the personality and always protect the individual.

In Greek mythology, there was a spirit called a *daimon*. The daimon was given to each man at birth by Zeus. The purpose of the spirit was to inspire, advise, guide, and protect the person throughout his life. In religion they were considered to be intermediary beings between the gods and men.

EARLY CHRISTIAN ACCEPTANCE

By the second century A.D., the concept of the guardian angel was widespread, outside of Scripture, and it has been ever since. The book, The Shepherd of Hermas, was widely accepted by the early Christians. Although it was never permitted into the canon of Scripture, it was bound in codex form with canonical literature, and read to the churches. The central figure was an angel who appeared to Hermas in the form of a shepherd. This book taught that each of us has two guardian angels — one good and the other evil.

> . . . There are two angels with man; one of righteousness, the other of iniquity.

> The angel of righteousness is mild and modest, and gentle, and quiet. When therefore, he gets into thy heart, immediately he talks with thee of righteousess, of modesty, of chastity, of bountifulness, of forgiveness, of charity, and piety.

When all these things come into thy heart, know then that the angel of righteousness is with thee. Wherefore harken to this angel and to his works.

Learn also the works of the angel of iniquity. He is first of all bitter, and angry, and foolish; and pernicious, and overthrows the servants of God. When therefore these things come into thy heart; thou shalt know by his works that this is the angel of iniquity [2 Hermas VI:7b, 9-11].

ORIGEN'S TEACHINGS

Origen was an early Christian philosopher and theologian. He was educated in Alexandria, Egypt in the third century. Origen taught that each person had his own guardian angel only as long as he remained faithful. This angel was supposed to have the power to protect the person from evil.

CATHOLIC DOCTRINE

The doctrine of the guardian angel is taught by most denominations, as well as both the Roman Catholic and the Eatern Orthodox religions. It is a belief that angels watch over children, protect individuals from harm, and guide them in the right way. The Pope authorized a celebration in honor of guardian angels to be observed each year on October 2. Catholics are also encouraged to pray to their guardian angels.

ISLAMIC TENET

Islam, one of the world's largest religions, teaches that each individual has four guardian angels. Two guard the person during the day and two at night. The angel on the right records the person's good works immediately. The one on the left writes down the evil acts a few hours later. The purpose of the delay is to allow the person an opportunity to repent before the wrong is counted against him.

The Koran is the sacred book of Islam, and its believers are called Muslims. The information for the Koran was supposed to have been received orally by Mohammed from the angel Gabriel and later put into writing by Mohammed's followers.

> It is alike whether you whisper or speak aloud, whether you hide under the cloak of night or walk about in broad day. Each has guardian angels before him and behind him, who watch him by Allah's command [Koran 13:19].

> As for those who say: "Our God is Allah," and take the right path to Him, the angels will descend to them, saying: "Let nothing alarm or grieve you. Rejoice in the Paradise you have been promised. We are your guardians in this world and in the next [Koran 41:30].

PHILOSOPHY/THEOLOGY

In the Middle Ages, theologians thought it necessary to "prove," by philosophical speculation, the existence of angels. This effort seems to us to be altogether unnecessary. Thomas Acquinas was born in Italy in 1227 and died when he was forty-seven years of age. Less than fifty years later he was canonized, or declared a saint, by the Roman Catholic Church.

One of Acquinas' most famous works is the **Summa Theologica.** The following excerpts are taken from FIRST PART QUESTION CXIII:

> ARTICLE 1. Whether Men are Guarded by the Angels?
> ... It is moreover manifest that as regards things to be done human knowledge and affection can vary and fail from good in many ways. And so it was necessary that angels should be assigned for the guardianship of men, in order to regulate them and move them to good.

> ARTICLE 2. Whether Each Man Is Guarded by an Angel?
> ... Each man has a guardian angel appointed to him. The reason for this is that the guardianship of angels belongs to the execution of Divine Providence concerning men.

ARTICLE 3. Whether to Guard Men Belongs Only to the Lowest Order of Angels?

. . . man is guarded in two ways. In one way by particular guardianship, according as to each man an angel is appointed to guard him; and such guardianship belongs to the lowest order of the angels. . .

ARTICLE 4. Whether Angels are Appointed to the Guardianship of All Men?

. . . an angel guardian is assigned to each man as long as he is a wayfarer. When, however, he arrives at the end of life, he no longer has a guardian angel, but in the kingdom he will have an angel to reign with him, in hell a demon to punish him.

ARTICLE 5. Whether an Angel Is Appointed to Guard a Man from His Birth?

. . . there are two opinions on this matter. For some have held that the guardian angel is appointed at the time of baptism, others, that he is appointed at the time of birth. . . .it can be said with some degree of probability, that the angel who guards the mother guards the child while in the womb. But at its birth, when it becomes separate from the mother, an angel guardian is appopinted to it. . . .

ARTICLE 6. Whether the Angel Guardian Ever Forsakes a Man?

. . . the angel guardian never forsakes a man entirely, but sometimes he leaves him in some particular, for instance by not preventing him from being subject to some trouble, or even falling into sin. . .

ARTICLE 7. Whether Angels Grieve for the Ills of Those Whom They Guard?

. . . Angels do not grieve, either for sins or for the pains inflicted on men. For grief and sorrow. . .are for those things which occur against our will. But nothing happens in the world contrary to the will of the angels and the other blessed. . .

Mortimer J. Adler in his book, *The Angels and Us*, points out that Acquinas created *Summa Theologica* without benefit of a Divine revelation. Neither does he refer to Catholic doctrine, much less the Scripture.

GUARDIAN ANGELS OF NATIONS

There is an ancient Jewish doctrine that nations have guardian angels and the Jews claimed Michael as the guardian angel of Israel. In ancient times, the pagan doctrine of polytheism taught the acceptance of multiple gods. In this teaching, each nation had its own separate god. With the elaboration of this principle, the guardian angel replaced the lesser god. It was imagined that Jehovah God appointed these guardian angels to administrate the interests of the country. The concept of personal guardian angels developed in a similar way.

GOD DEALT WITH MANY NATIONS

The following passages of Scripture illustrate the fact that God dealt with many nations and kings who had their gods.

But if serving the LORD seems undesirable to you, then choose for yourselves this day whom you will serve, whether the gods your forefathers served beyond the River, or the gods of the Amorites, in whose land you are living. But as for me and my household, we will serve the LORD [Joshua 24:15].

Kings came, they fought; the kings of Canaan fought at Taanach by the waters of Megiddo, but they carried off no silver, no plunder. From the heavens the stars fought, from their courses they fought against Sisera [Judges 5:19-20].

In that day the LORD will punish the powers in the heavens above and the kings on the earth below [Isaiah 24:21].

"I said, 'You are "gods"; you are all sons of the Most High.' But you will die like mere men; you will fall like every other ruler." Rise up, O God, judge the earth, for all the nations are your inheritance [Psalm 82:6-8].

ANGELS OF PERSIA AND GREECE?

Daniel referred to the princes of Persia and Greece in Daniel 10-12. Michael, who is the archangel, is also called a prince. Some would interpret this to mean the prince of Persia was the guardian angel of Persia, because later Judaism accredited protecting angels to national groups. The princes or angels of Persia and Greece were hindering God's angels. Gabriel, Michael and another angel clearly acted in God's interest in Daniel 8-12.

But the prince of the Persian kingdom resisted me twenty-one days. Then Michael, one of the chief princes, came to help me, because I was detained there with the king of Persia [Daniel 10:13].

So he said, "Do you know why I have come to you? Soon I will return to fight against the prince of Persia, and when I go, the prince of Greece will come; but first I will tell you what is written in the Book of Truth. (No one supports me against them except Michael, your prince. . . [Daniel 10:20-21].

NATIONAL GUARDIAN ANGEL IN SCRIPTURE?

The most direct biblical basis from which the belief in a guardian angel for each nation evolved, originates in the following verses.

And when you look up to the sky and see the sun, the moon and the stars — all the heavenly array — do not be enticed into bowing down to them and worshiping things the LORD your God has apportioned to all the nations under heaven [Deuteronomy 4:19].

When the Most High gave the nations their inheritance, when he divided all mankind, he set up boundaries for the peoples according to the number of the sons of Israel [Deuteronomy 32:8].

By the translation of the Septuagint Version the idea of the guardian angels of nations had its beginning.

. . . he established the bounds of the nations according to the number of the angels of God [Deuteronomy 32:8, Septuagint Version].

From this time the many nations were portrayed as having their own particular guardian angels. By the second century B.C., there was far-reaching acceptance of the belief in national angelic guardians.

ADDITIONAL INFORMATION

The fourteen apocryphal books were never a part of the Hebrew Scriptures, but were included in the Greek version which is called the Septuagint. They were not separated from the inspired books until the Coverdale Bible was printed in 1535. Coverdale placed them between the Old and New Testaments with an introductory explanation that they were less authoritative. They were not omitted from the English translations of the Bible until 1699. Today they are included in the Bibles used by Catholics, Episcopalians, and Lutherans. Apocryphal books, though uninspired, can provide a valuable source of historical information. They are also responsible for contributing misleading information.

SUMMARY

It is obvious that the belief in personal and national guardian angels existed among the Jews after the Exile, and in the early church. We can see that their source of information on the subject was not the one source which we accept as authoritative — the books of Scripture.

Scripture does not support the concept of the guardian angel. We have many examples of God's people being guarded, delivered, and assured by angels. In ancient times God used the operation of angels to influence and protect people. Scriptures, however, do not teach the appointment, at birth or at any other time, of a specific angel to guard an individual.

There is no record in Scripture of an angel who was sent to a person on earth in the role we have described as "the guardian angel." There is no reason to believe that God ever used this system, the guardian angel, to protect individuals. The dependence of a Christian upon an angel for any form of preservation or guidance is contrary to the teaching of the New Testament.

This in no way lessens God's concern for us or diminishes His power and ability to protect us. It was, however, not His design to utilize an angel as the guardian and personal defender of every Jew, or every faithful Christian, or any person on earth.

REVIEW

1. Name some biblical characters who were protected by angels._____

   _____

2. According to tradition, who receives a guardian angel?   When?_____

3. What is the assumed purpose of the guardian angel?

   _____

4. What service is a guardian angel supposed to perform?_____

5. Does Scripture teach the ministry of guardian angels?

   ___ _____

6. Name some sources which teach the existence of guardian angels. _____

7. Did God appoint national guardian angels?_____

   _____

8. Do you have a guardian angel? _____

NOTES

_____
_____
_____
_____
_____
_____
_____
_____
_____
_____
_____

Chapter Thirteen

Evil Angels

H aving surveyed the biblical teaching on angels who serve God, we shall now consider two categories of wicked angels who are found in Scripture. These two distinct groups are God's angels who sinned and Satan's angels. To aid our study, an investigation of demons and demon-possession is also included. Then we shall consider the origin of Satan and attempt to answer the question, "Is Satan a fallen angel?"

ANGELS WHO SINNED

The first group we shall study is the angels who sinned. God through Christ created good angels (John 1:1-3). He created them to serve as messengers and ministering spirits. They had the ability to choose between right and wrong. Some of them made the wrong choice, they sinned and were sent to hell. These sinful angels were mentioned indirectly by Peter and Jude, where they were used as examples of God's punishment of sin.

> For if God did not spare angels when they sinned, but sent them to hell, putting them into gloomy dungeons to be held for judgment; . . .if this is so, then the Lord knows how to rescue Godly men from trials and to hold the unrighteous for the day of judgment, while continuing their punishment [2 Peter 2:4,9].

Though the exact nature of their sin is unknown, we are told how the angels were punished. In the Greek, the

190

verb *tartaroo* which is translated "cast down to hell" indicates the place which the Greeks called Tartarus. They used this word to describe the place where the unrighteous awaited God's judgment. It is impossible to leave this region because "a great chasm has been fixed" [Luke 16:26].

The letter of Jude adds information to the investigation of angels who sinned. Jude wrote to warn against false teachers. He cited occasions when sin was punished, and one of those was the sin of angels.

> And the angels who did not keep their positions of authority but abandoned their own home — these he has kept in darkness, bound with everlasting chains for judgment on the great Day [Jude verse 6].

Perhaps the angels were appointed certain areas or assignments. These angels did not stay in their place, or did not fulfill their responsibilities. Some would identify this sin with the "sons of God" in Genesis 6.

> When men began to increase in number on the earth and daughters were born to them, the sons of God saw that the daughters of men were beautiful, and they married any of them they chose [Genesis 6:1-2].

The questionable part of this theory is: who are "the sons of God" in this passage? The same phrase *(bene elohim)* was used three times in the Book of Job. Each of these was a reference to angels. From the context in Genesis, however, it appears that the "sons of God" were the good descendants of Seth, and the "daughters of men" were the evil descendants of Cain.

This is a logical interpretation of the text. The following explanation is not meant to discredit this understanding, but to explore another possible meaning of the passage.

When attempting to prove that "the sons of God" were men and not angels, one usually makes the point that angels do not marry, which assumes that sexual relations are not possible for angels.

> At the resurrection people will neither marry nor be given in marriage; they will be like the angels in heaven [Matthew 22:30].

This verse, however, refers to "the angels in heaven," while Jude verse 6 told us that some angels "abandoned their own home." Circumstances on earth would not correspond to those in heaven. For instance, since angels are spirit beings, it is not reasonable to assume that in heaven they eat the food of mortals. They did, however, eat mortal food when they visited Abraham on earth.

> He then brought some curds and milk and the calf that had been prepared, and set these before them. While they ate, he stood near them under a tree [Genesis 18:8].

It should be considered as a possibility that "the sons of God" in Genesis 6, as in Job, were angels. The offspring of this union were called the Nephilim. They were giants, "heros of old, men of renown" [Genesis 6:4], but the Hebrew word means "fallen ones."

We cannot be certain what their sin was, but these angels were mentioned by Job's friend, Eliphaz, in a comparison of angelic and human accountability for sin.

> If God places no trust in his servants, if he charges his angels with error, how much more those who live in houses of clay... [Job 4:18-19a].

Do not confuse the angels who sinned with the wicked angels of Satan. The angels who sinned were created by God and were originally good, but later they chose to do evil. They were punished by being sent to hell and chained in gloomy, dark dungeons to await judgment.

ANGELS OF SATAN

A group which is entirely separate from the sinful angels who are confined to hell, is Satan's angels, or the devil's angels. Just as the good angls are spirit beings who are servants of God, Satan's angels are evil spirits who serve the devil. The origin of these angels is unknown.

We find two references to this group of angels in the New Testament.

> Then he will say to those on his left, "Depart from me, you who are cursed, into the eternal fire prepared for the devil and his angels" [Matthew 25:41].

The angels of Satan were discussed here in an indirect manner. Jesus was teaching His disciples concerning the kingdom of heaven. In the parable of the sheep and the goats, He taught the rewards to the virtuous would be "the kingdom prepared for you since the creation of the world." The opposite of these were the ones who were cursed. They would be sent to a place not prepared for men but for "the devil and his angels."

> And there was war in heaven. Michael and his angels fought against the dragon, and the dragon and his angels fought back. But he was not strong enough, and they lost their place in heaven. The great dragon was hurled down—that ancient serpent called the devil, or Satan, who leads the whole world astray. He was hurled to the earth, and his angels with him [Revelation 12:7-9].

The vision which John described in the Revelation used symbols to represent the incidents it prophesied. The dragon was a visualization of Satan and his evil influence evident in the Roman Empire. When Satan's angels were thrown to earth, it was their defeat, not their beginning.

John described the action of the dragon he saw in the vision.

> His tail swept a third of the stars out of the sky and flung them to the earth [Revelation 12:4a].

This activity symbolized the defeat of the evil rulers who persecuted God's people. The dragon represented Satan but this description was his defeat, through the downfall of the evil Roman Empire, not his start. There is no evidence to support the assumption that this vision depicted the beginning of Satan or his angels.

We have no biblical facts on the origin of Satan's angels. There is, however, information available from other sources. The Church of Jesus Christ of Latter-day Saints, sometimes called the Mormons, teaches a definite origin of Satan's angels. 2 Nephi, which is in the Book of Mormon, said that those who followed Satan became the devil's angels.

... and we become devils, angels to a devil, to be shut out from the presence of our God, and to remain with the father of lies, in misery like unto himself... [2 Nephi 9:9].

DEMONS

In the synagogue there was a man possessed by a demon, an evil spirit. He cried out at the top of his voice... [Luke 4:33].

The demons were the spirit messengers of Satan. In the New Testament, the words "demon" and "evil spirit" are used as synonyms. During the time that Christ was here on earth, demon-possession was a distinct activity of Satan. This type of activity did not exist in the Old Testament.

Demons in the New Testament had the ability and power to bring harm to human beings. They were able to take possession of bodies and inflict injuries. These demons sometimes caused the loss of speech, sight, and sanity. They affected children as well as adults, in some instances bringing about seizures and convulsions. In spite of these physical symptoms, those who were demon-possessed were separate from those with sickness or disease. The Scriptures deal with demon-possession as a distinct category.

News about him spread all over Syria, and people brought to him all who were ill with various diseases, those suffering severe pain, the demon-possessed, those having seizures, and the paralyzed, and he healed them [Matthew 4:24].

They drove out many demons and anointed many sick people with oil and healed them [Mark 6:13].

... and also some women who had been cured of evil spirits and diseases: Mary (called Magdalene) from whom seven demons had come out... [Luke 8:2].

Jesus possessed power and authority over these demons so that they responded to His command.

Jesus rebuked the demon, and it came out of the boy, and he was healed from that moment [Matthew 17:18].

The apostles were given power by Jesus and the ability to triumph over demons. The authority they received from Jesus made them able to expel the evil spirits just as He did.

Calling the twelve to him, he sent them out two by two and gave them authority over evil spirits [Mark 6:7].

Jesus also extended the power over demons to the seventy-two disciples whom He sent out in pairs to go ahead of Him to the places He visited. Luke recorded Jesus' conversation with His disciples about the success of their mission. They reported to Him that they were victorious in defeating demons. Jesus said that He saw Satan fall from heaven.

After this the Lord appointed seventy-two others and sent them two by two ahead of him to every town and place where he was about to go [Luke 10:1].

The seventy-two returned with joy and said, "Lord, even the demons submit to us in your name."
He replied, "I saw Satan fall like lightning from heaven" [Luke 10:17-18].

Did Jesus tell His followers that Satan was originally an angel? No! The demons were the representatives of Satan and the enemies of Christ. Therefore, He visualized the disciples victory over evil symbolically, as if Satan were cast out of heaven. Jesus was speaking in a figurative manner of the defeat experienced by Satan when His disciples triumphed over demons. The context of their discussion was contemporary with the time Christ lived on earth. It would have been inconsistent for Him to start a discussion on the origin of Satan at this particular time.

During the time of Christ, possession by demons or evil spirits was widespread. Demon-possession was not recorded after the time of the Book of Acts. The activity of demons provided an opportunity for Jesus and His followers to demonstrate God's power over evil. When the miraculous age ended (1 Corinthians 13:8-10), there was no longer a supernatural remedy available. Demons had served their purpose. Satan's power was curtailed by Jesus' triumph over death (Revelation 12:10-12). The affliction of demon-possession disappeared.

Demons were the agents of Satan. He sent these evil spirits to possess the minds and bodies of numbers of human beings. These angels of Satan represented him in a way comparable to the angel messengers used by God. The angels of Satan no longer use miraculous action just as the angels of God have ceased to be involved with us in a supernatural manner.

PAUL'S MESSENGER OF SATAN

Paul suffered from a handicap which is not identified in Scripture. He referred to it as his "thorn," and asked God three times to relieve this affliction. Many people speculate as to what Paul's disability may have been. We know from his second letter to the Corinthians that Paul regarded the ailment as the work of an evil angel.

> To keep me from becoming conceited because of these surpassingly great revelations, there was given me a thorn in my flesh, a messenger of Satan, to torment me [2 Corinthians 12:7].

The exact nature of Paul's affliction was not revealed in the Bible, therefore it continues to be unknown.

SATAN

There is widespread belief in the world today that the devil himself is a "fallen angel." This opinion is so well-known that we cannot exclude Satan from our study of angels. We shall first explore the Scriptures regarding Satan and then examine the myth of Satan's origin. This examination will show that we have been guided to misinterpret the Scripture.

The Hebrew word which is translated *satan,* has the meaning "an adversary." When used with "the," it is defined "the adversary," or "the satan." In the Book of Job, the word which was translated "Satan," was always preceded by "the" in Hebrew. In Chronicles, the role of Satan was more clearly defined. He was no longer *the adversary,* but *adversary* translated with a capital letter "S". The proper name *Satan* does not appear in the Old Testament until

196

1 Chronicles, and is found only in this book and two others — Job and Zechariah.

> One day the angels came to present themselves before the Lord, and Satan also came with them [Job 1:6].
>
> On another day the angels came to present themselves before the Lord, and Satan also came with them to present himself before him [Job 2:1].
>
> The Lord said to Satan, "Very well, then, everything he has is in your hands, but on the man himself do not lay a finger." Then Satan went out from the presence of the Lord [Job 1:12].
>
> The Lord said to Satan, "Very well, then, he is in your hands; but you must spare his life" [Job 2:6].

Satan appeared here in the role of the prosecutor of Job. God limited and controlled what Satan was allowed to inflict on Job which indicates God's authority over Satan.

In the Old Testament the word was also used to refer to human adversaries, but in the New Testament it was used only as the proper name of the devil. Just as there was a developing doctrine of angels, there was also an expanding of the teaching concerning Satan. This increase occurred as Satan expanded his efforts to exert an evil influence on God's people. In the Greek language, *satanas* was derived from the Aramaic and means "an adversary." In the New Testament it referred to "Satan the adversary of God and Christ."

In the New Testament, Satan was charged as an adversary of Peter. Jesus warned Peter because He knew that Peter would deny Him.

> "Simon, Simon, Satan has asked to sift you as wheat. But I have prayed for you, Simon, that your faith may not fail. And when you have turned back, strengthen your brothers" [Luke 22:31-32].

Satan asked for Peter as earlier he had asked for Job. Satan was not allowed to test Peter without God's permission. This was another example of God's authority to limit Satan's power.

The names "the devil" and "Satan" were used synonymously in the New Testament. In relating the facts of Jesus' temptation by Satan, Matthew called him "the tempter" or "the devil." Later, when Jesus spoke to him He called Satan by name.

The tempter came to him and said, "If you are the Son of God, tell these stones to become bread."

Then the devil took him to the holy city and had him stand on the highest point of the temple.

Jesus said to him, "Away from me Satan! For it is written: 'Worship the Lord your God, and serve him only' " [Matthew 4:3, 5, 10].

John recorded the events which occurred in the upper room. This was another instance of the names "the devil" and "Satan" being synonymous. We learn early in the account that "the devil" was responsible for what Judas would do. While Jesus and Judas were eating together, Satan took control of him.

The evening meal was being served, and the devil had already prompted Judas Iscariot, son of Simon, to betray Jesus.

As soon as Judas took the bread, Satan entered into him. "What you are about to do, do quickly," Jesus told him [John 13:2, 27].

Paul wrote to the Corinthians to warn against false teachers or "false apostles." He described the trickery of these men who mask themselves as "apostles of Christ." As a further example, he also said that Satan disguises himself "as an angel of light."

For such men are false apostles, deceitful workmen, masquerading as apostles of Christ. And no wonder, for Satan himself masquerades as an angel of light. It is not surprising, then, if his servants masquerade as servants of righteousness. Their end will be what their actions deserve [2 Corinthians 11:13-15].

Paul did not say that Satan was once an angel of light who sinned against God and became the devil.

John described a vision in which the dragon and Satan were symbolic of the paganism of the Roman Empire.

Their being cast down to earth was representative of Christ's victory and their final exclusion.

> But he was not strong enough, and they lost their place in heaven. The great dragon was hurled down — that ancient serpent called the devil, or Satan, who leads the whole world astray. He was hurled to the earth and his angels with him [Revelation 12:8-9].

> He seized the dragon, that ancient serpent, who is the devil, or Satan, and bound him for a thousand years [Revelation 20:2].

John also used the terms "devil" and "Satan" synonmously and represented Satan symbolically as the "dragon" and the "ancient serpent." He did not speak of the origin of Satan but rather the defeat of Satan.

ORIGIN OF SATAN

Many people have gone in search of the origin of Satan. Some believe that both God and Satan have always existed, that they are equal in power, and in ability to influence the universe. Those who reject this theory anxiously seek to uncover the initial source of evil. They seem to think that the absence of this knowledge makes Satan equal with God. There is no biblical answer to the question—"What is the origin of Satan?" There is only one possible answer—"The origin of Satan is not revealed in Scripture." By failing to establish an origin for Satan we are not endorsing his equality with God.

To escape this theory, people continued to strive frantically for an explanation of Satan's origin. This produced the theory that God created Satan. We all decline this possibility because we are reluctant to have God be the creator of evil. Thus, out of desperation the perfect solution was fabricated: that God created Lucifer, a good angel with free moral agency, or the ability to choose. That angel chose to sin, God punished him, and the result was, Lucifer became Satan. We know that angels sinned and were sent to hell, but those angels were imprisoned and held for judgment. It is not plausible to conceive of Satan as the leader of those sinful angels who are imprisoned. The origin of Satan remains unknown.

LUCIFER

Was Lucifer the leader of the angels who sinned? There is a traditional belief that an archangel who sinned against God, was sent from heaven with a number of other rebellious angels. The story goes that Lucifer and his followers became Satan and his angels. This is more than just a traditional belief, it has become accepted as authorized doctrine. The conclusion was the result of a misinterpretation of Scripture and an urgent desire to explain the origin of Satan. Was Satan Lucifer, an angel who sinned? Nowhere does the Bible teach that there was an angel named Lucifer, much less that he became Satan as the result of sin.

The angels who sinned are chained in dungeons, awaiting judgment (2 Peter 2:4; Jude verse 6). Thus, we find no similarity between the angels who sinned and Satan. It is unreasonable that Satan would be allowed to enter God's presence at will (Job 1:6; 2:1), if he were a defiant angel who had been expelled from heaven and sent to hell.

ISAIAH AND THE KING OF BABYLON

One scriptural reference which is supposed to explain the origin of Satan is Isaiah 14:12-15

How you have fallen from heaven,
O morning star, son of the dawn!
You have been cast down to the earth,
you who once laid low the nations!
You said in your heart,
"I will ascend to heaven;
I will raise my throne
above the stars of God;
I will sit enthroned on the mount of assembly,
on the utmost heights of the sacred mountain.
I will ascend above the tops of the clouds;
I will make myself like the Most High."
But you are brought down to the grave.
to the depths of the pit.

This was clearly a description of the fall of the king of Babylon. Isaiah wrote to warn Judah that she would be captured and exiled by the Babylonians. In this work of prophecy chapters 13 and 14 were a writing against Babylon and the Babylonian king.

An oracle concering Babylon that Isaiah son of Amoz saw: [Isaiah 13:1].

. . . you will take up this taunt against the king of Babylon: How the oppressor has come to an end! How his fury has ended! [Isaiah 14:4].

It was not left to readers to imagine or wonder who was under discussion in this passage. It is specifically stated for all to read.

The King James Version translated the Hebrew word for "morning-star" as "Lucifer." This unfortunate interpretation dates back to the fifth century. Jerome, 340-420 A.D., was a Bible scholar of the Roman Catholic Church, a writer and historian. He translated the Old Testament from Hebrew into Latin. This version, the Vulgate, was completed in 405 A.D. When Jerome translated Isaiah 14:12, he gave the interpretation "lucifer" to the Hebrew word which means "day-star" or "morning-star." Jerome was the first to apply the name "Lucifer" to Satan. It was accepted at the time and went on unquestioned for a thousand years.

A comparison of the Isaiah passage, as seen in several translations may help us to understand how this misleading interpretation has been improved in later versions.

How art thou fallen from heaven, O Lucifer, son of the morning! how art thou cut down to the ground which didst weaken the nations! (KJV 1611).

How have you fallen from heaven, O day star, son of the morning! how art thou cut down to the ground, that didst lay low the nations! (ASV 1901).

How you have fallen from heaven,
    O morning star, son of the dawn!

You have been cast down to the earth
    you who once laid low the nations! (NIV 1978).

Jack P. Lewis, wrote in the *Gospel Advocate* in 1987 suggesting that difficulty with this passage may also result from faulty cross-references. The Bible study aids which are supplied by the editor are not placed by inspiration. There is a risk that the cross-reference will suggest a defective connection. When the King James Version was published in 1611, it was not furnished with cross-references. Although they are intended to be helpful, they can be misleading. Such is the case when Isaiah 14:12 directs the reader to Luke 10:18 and Revelation 12:8-9 ("The Value and Danger of Bible Cross-References," CXXIX, (1987).

EZEKIEL AND THE RULER OF TYRE

Ezekiel was a prophet during the Exile in Babylon. God gave Ezekiel a judgment against seven different countries. One of these nations was Tyre, and a prophecy against her ruler was included. This Scripture has also been mis-applied to Satan.

> The word of the Lord came to me: "Son of man, take up a lament concerning the king of Tyre and say to him: 'This is what the Sovereign Lord says:
>
> " 'You were the model of perfection,
>   full of wisdom and perfect in beauty.
> You were in Eden, the garden of God;
> every precious stone adorned you:
>   ruby, topaz and emerald,
>   chrysolite, onyx and jasper,
>   sapphire, turquoise and beryl.
> Your settings and mountings were made of gold;
>   on the day you were created they were prepared.
> You were anointed as a guardian cherub,
>   for so I ordained you.
> You were on the holy mount of God;
>   you walked among the fiery stones.
> You were blameless in your ways
>   from the day you were created
>   till wickedness was found in you' " [Ezekiel 28:11-15].

Could this apply to Satan, the devil? No! Was he blameless from his creation? John 8:44 says that the devil "was a murderer from the beginning," and in 1 John 3:8, "the devil has been sinning from the beginning."

> " 'Through your widespread trade
>   you were filled with violence, and you sinned.
> So I drove you in disgrace from the mount of God,
>   and I expelled you, O guardian cherub,
>   from among the fiery stones.
> Your heart became proud
>   on account of your beauty,
> and you corrupted your wisdom
>   because of your splendor.
> So I threw you to the earth;
>   I made a spectacle of you before kings.
> By your many sins and dishonest trade
>   you have desecrated your sanctuaries.
> So I made a fire come out from you,
>   and it consumed you,
> and I reduced you to ashes on the ground
>   in the sight of all who were watching.
> All the nations who knew you
>   are appalled at you;
> you have come to a horrible end
>   and will be no more' " [Ezekiel 28:16-19].

Do these verses relate to Satan? No! If he were consumed by fire and reduced to ashes, Satan would have been destroyed with the fulfillment of Ezekiel's prophecy. Of course, we know this did not happen, because we read of Satan's activity throughout the New Testament.

This teaching against the ruler of Tyre corresponds to the prophecy of Isaiah against the Babylonian king. Ezekiel 32 is an outcry against the Egyptian Pharaoh. Does this prophecy against an evil ruler also teach of Satan?

We cannot use the Scripture to prove the lineage and derivation of Satan. The Bible is not specific concerning the beginning or source of this evil being. Although this knowledge is not accessible to us in inspired writing, there is abundant information available from other sources.

THE SECRETS OF ENOCH/ORIGIN OF SATAN

The Secrets of Enoch, or 2 Enoch, is thought to have been written about the beginning of the Christian age, or the first century A.D. and was accredited to Enoch. The knowledge that this book ever existed was lost to us for hundreds of years, but it was available to early Christians and undoubtedly had an influence on them. Books such as this are known as Pseudepigrapha, which means falsely ascribed. This was written long after the lifetime of Enoch, the Old Testament personality who was carried away without experiencing death. The author claimed that God took him to heaven and showed him the works of creation.

> And from the rock I cut off a great fire, and from the fire I created the orders of the incorporeal ten troops of angels, and their weapons are fiery and their raiment a burning flame, and I commanded that each one should stand in his order. And one from out the order of angels, having turned away with the order that was under him, conceived an impossible thought, to place his throne higher than the clouds above the earth, that he might become equal in rank to my power. And I threw him out from the height with his angels, and he was flying in the air continuously above the bottomless [2 Enoch XXIX:2-4].

HAGGADAH/ORIGIN OF SATAN

The Jewish tradition of storytelling and biblical commentary, or interpretation of oral law was called *Haggadah*. It was similar to religious fiction and developed legend by embellishing the Scripture. According to the Haggadah, the angels were jealous of Adam. God wanted the angels to show reverence to Adam, but Satan refused.

> Satan, the greatest of the angels in heaven, with twelve wings, instead of six like all the others, refused to pay heed to the behest of God, . . .

God agreed to give Adam and Satan a test. He would see which one of them could call the animals by the correct names. Satan failed and Adam succeeded. Satan still refused to admit Adam's excellence, and he influenced a large number of angels to join him. The first to bow down to Adam was the angel Michael who wished, by example, to lead the other angels.

Michael addressed Satan: "Give adoration to the image of God! But if you do not, then the Lord God will break out in wrath against you." Satan replied: "If he breaks out in wrath against me, I will exalt my throne above the stars of God, I will be like the Most High!" At once God flung Satan and his host out of Heaven, down to the earth, and from that moment dates the enmity between Satan and man [Louis Ginzburg, *The Legend of the Jews*].

GOSPEL OF BARTHOLOMEW/ORIGIN OF SATAN

The Gospel of Bartholomew was a Christian book of questionable authority, written about the 3rd century. It described Beliar (Satan) who revealed to Bartholomew how he was thrown down from heaven.

. . . Then the earth was shaken and Beliar came up, held by six hundred sixty angels and bound with fiery chains.

He was sixteen hundred yards long and forty yards broad. His face was like a lightning of fire, and his eyes like sparks, and from his nostrils came a stinking smoke. His mouth was like a cleft of rock and a single one of his wings was eighty yards long. . .

. . ."If you wish to know my name, I was first called Satanael, which means 'angel of God.' But when I rejected the image of God, I was called Satan, which means 'angel of Hell.' "

. . .Michael said to me: "Worship the image of God which he has made in his own likeness."

But I said: "I am fire of fire. I was the first angel to be formed, and shall I worship clay and matter?"

And Michael said to me: "Worship lest God be angry with you."

I answered: "God will not be angry with me, but I will set up my throne, and shall be as he is." Then God was angry with me and cast me down after he had commanded the windows of heaven to be opened.

When I was thrown down, he asked the six hundred angels that stood under me whether they would worship Adam. They replied: "As we saw our leader do, we also will not worship him who is less than ourselves" (*New Testament Apocrypha*, vol. 1].

ISLAMIC ORIGIN OF SATAN

The sacred book of the religion of Islam, the Koran, also taught the origin of Satan. The Koran taught that in a contest of knowledge, angels lost to Adam. Iblis, who had formerly held an exalted position, refused to honor the first man, thus he fell from favor. The Koran interpreted his disobedience as the sin of pride. Thus, Iblis and some of the angels are believed to have fallen from their place with Allah because of rebellion.

We created man from dry clay, from black moulded loam, and before him Satan from smokeless fire. Your Lord said to the angels: "I am creating man from dry clay, from black moulded loam. When I have fashioned him and breathed of My spirit into him, kneel down and prostrate yourselves before him."

All the angels prostrated themselves, except Satan. He refused to prostrate himself.

"Satan," said Allah, "why do you not prostrate yourself?"

He replied, "I will not bow to a mortal created of dry clay, or black moulded loam."

"Begone," said Allah, "you are accursed. My curse shall be on you till Judgment-day" [Koran 15:28-34].

MILTON AND DANTE/ORIGIN OF SATAN

You will remember that we considered Milton's *Paradise Lost* in our observation of the effect of literature on our concept of the angels. Milton wrote that Satan was formerly an angel who wanted to be equal with God. This sin of pride caused God to cast him out of heaven, along with the angels who supported him.

Another of the great works of literature which we believe had an affect on the perception of angels is Dante's *Divine Comedy*. This classic poem also added to the list of information about the mythical origin of Satan. Dante gave little detail of the fall of Satan, but he alluded to Satan having been a beautiful angel who rebelled against God. According to Canto 34 of the portion called "Hell," when Satan fell down from heaven, the earth was so frightened that the Mount of Purgatory rose up out of the water. Although his specific information about the origin of Satan is brief, Dante described Satan and his predicament in hell in great detail.

THOMAS ACQUINAS/ORIGIN OF SATAN

The theologian-philosopher, Thomas Acquinas, contributed his influence to this subject with as much assurance as he did to the guardian angel question. His speculation enabled him to determine that angels were created good, with free will to choose between good and evil. Some of the angels sinned because they pursued good in the wrong way, wanting to be like God and this was their pride. Acquinas concluded that the devil was at one time the highest angel and that he caused the other angels to sin.

CHURCH OF JESUS CHRIST of LATTER-DAY SAINTS/ ORIGIN OF SATAN

The Mormons assume that Revelation 12:9 was the birth of the devil. The Doctrine and Covenants, Section 29, claims to be a revelation given through Joseph Smith in 1830. It taught that the devil and his angels were cast out of heaven to tempt man.

And it came to pass that Adam, being tempted of the devil—for behold the devil was before Adam, for he rebelled against me saying, Give me thine honor, which is my power; and also a third part of the hosts of heaven turned he away from me because of their agency; And they were thrust down, and thus came the devil and his angels. [Doctrine and Covenants 29:36-37].

Section 76 described a vision which Joseph Smith and Sidney Rigdon saw in 1832. It informed them that an angel of God fell and became the devil.

And this we saw also and bear record, that an angel of God who was in authority in the presence of God, who rebelled against the Only Begotten Son whom the Father loved and who was in the bosom of the Father, was thrust down from the presence of God and the Son, And was called Perdition, for the heavens wept over him — he was Lucifer, a son of the morning [Doctrine and Covenants 76:25-26].

The Pearl of Great Price is the title of a volume which the latter-day saints consider to be Scripture. Joseph Smith began his own translation of the Bible in June, 1830. The Book of Moses contains the revelations Smith received to restore the truths which Mormons claim had been lost from the Bible. Chapter four told how Satan became the devil. He asked God to send him instead of the "Only Begotten" to redeem mankind.

Wherefore, because that Satan rebelled against me, and sought to destroy the agency of man, which I, the Lord God had given him, and also, that I should give unto him mine own power; by the power of mine Only Begotten, I caused that he should be cast down; And he became Satan, yea, even the devil, the father of all lies, to deceive and to blind men and to lead them captive at his will, even as many as would not hearken unto my voice [Moses 4:3-4].

JEHOVAH'S WITNESSES/ORIGIN OF SATAN

The religious organization known as Jehovah's Witnesses is one of the largest publishers of printed material in the world today. The book, *You Can Live Forever in Paradise on Earth*, was published by the Watchtower Bible and Tract Society of New York, Inc. This volume provides very specific information regarding

"WHO THE DEVIL IS" (pp. 19-20). He was said to have been created by God as an angel who was good and later sinned and became Satan.

> The angel that became the devil was present when God created the earth and later the first human couple, Adam and Eve (Job 38:4,7). So he would have heard God tell them to have children (Genesis 1:27,28). He knew that after a while the whole earth would be filled with righteous people worshiping God. That was God's purpose. However this angel thought a great deal of his own beauty and intelligence and wanted to receive for himself the worship that would be given to God (Ezekiel 28:13-15; Matthew 4:10). Instead of putting this wrong desire out of his mind, he kept thinking about it. This led to his taking action to obtain the honor and importance he desired. What did he do?—James 1:14-15.

> The rebellious angel used a lowly serpent to speak to the first woman, Eve. He did this much as a skilled person can make it seem as if a nearby animal or dummy figure is talking. But it was really this rebellious angel, the one called in the Bible "the original serpent," who was speaking to Eve (Revelation 12:9). He said that God was not telling her the truth, and holding back from her knowledge that she should have (Genesis 3:1-5). This was a hateful lie and it made him a devil. He thus became also an opposer of God, or a Satan. As you can see, it is wrong to think of the Devil as a creature with horns and a pitchfork who oversees some underground place of torment. He is really a very powerful, but wicked angel.

SUMMARY

God created angels who were good, but having free moral agency, some later sinned. He sent them to hell where they are chained in darkness to wait for judgment. There is a remote possibility that the "sons of God" in Genesis 6, referred to these angels. It is, however, more likely that this was a reference to the descendants of Seth.

In Job, Matthew, and Revelation, the devil's angels were mentioned. Demons and evil spirits played an important role in the New Testament. Jesus and those whom He authorized, had the power to dispossess the demons. When the miraculous cure was no longer available, possession by demons ceased. The demons were a form of Satan's angels.

Satan means "adversary" and was used with "the" (the satan) until the time of Chronicles. By then he was personified and had the proper name, "Satan." Isaiah and Ezekiel wrote against evil rulers, they did not describe the origin of Satan. John depicted Satan as a dragon in his symbolic vision, where he described the defeat, not the source of Satan.

A misleading translation in the Vulgate, by Jerome, led to the building up of a legend about Lucifer. He was thought to be a special angel who sinned against God, was thrown out of heaven, and became Satan. There is no angel named Lucifer in Scripture. Jesus did not teach that Satan originated in heaven.

Many nonbiblical sources are available to supply this information. The pseudepigraphal book of 2 Enoch, stated that one of the angels wanted to become equal to God in position and in power. The oral tradition and storytelling of the Jews supported the belief that Satan, who was the greatest of the angels, became jealous when God created Adam out of clay and required the angels to bow down to him. Satan lost a contest with Adam and in anger desired to be like God.

The Gospel of Bartholomew also taught that Satan was an angel who refused to worship God's new creature. He became envious and God threw him down along with six hundred angels. The Koran likewise taught that God required the angels to worship the first man. Satan refused and God cursed him.

The Mormons believe that parts of God's Word were lost or never revealed. Therefore, Joseph Smith and others received revelations to supplement the Bible. The Book of Mormon, The Pearl of Great Price, and Doctrine and Covenants contain this information. These books taught than an angel of God. Lucifer, rebelled against God and was sent out from heaven. He took a third of the good angels with him in the revolt and they became Satan and his angels.

Jehovah's Witnesses teach that Satan was originally a good angel, created by God, who sinned by lying to Eve. This angel wanted Adam and Eve to worship him instead of God. He tricked Eve by using a technique like ventriloquism to make the serpent speak to her. He was beautiful but became powerful and wicked.

The Scriptures do not provide detailed information concerning the origin of Satan or his angels. The biblical references to these beings are indirect in nature. This is in sharp contrast to the wealth of specific data which comes from other sources.

REVIEW

1. Name two categories of evil angels found in Scripture.
   _____

2. What is the origin of each of these groups of angels?
   _____

3. What were the demons we read about in the New Testament? _____

4. What is the meaning of the word "satan?"_____

5. What is the origin of Satan?_____
   _____

6. What is the correct translation of the word "lucifer?"
   _____

7. Name several sources outside Scripture which teach the origin of Satan._____
   _____

8. What does Islam teach is the origin of Satan?_____
   _____

9. How did Milton and Dante contribute to our confusion concerning Satan's origin?_____
   _____

10. Concerning the origin of Satan, Mormon doctrine teaches _____

_____

_____

11. How do Jehovah's Witnesses differ from the Scripture in their teaching of Satan's origin?_____

_____

NOTES

_____

_____

_____

_____

_____

_____

_____

_____

_____

_____

_____

_____

_____

_____

_____

_____

_____

_____

_____

_____

_____

_____

_____

_____

_____

_____

_____

_____

Conclusion

The word angel means "messenger." Angels are the creation of God through His Son Jesus Christ. This occurred some time before He created the world. The angels are too numerous to count, and the Bible does not classify them as male or female. They do not have marriage relationships, and they do not suffer death. Angels were used by God, as recorded in Scripture, in various functions. One of these, as the name implies, was to bring messages. They were also employed to administer God's will, both to His people and their enemies. The angels guided and protected people, ministered to those in distress, and interpreted visions and dreams.

Angels are in the presence of the Father in heaven where they praise and worship Him. They attend God's throne and witness His recognition of those who confess Him before men. It is in the presence of the angels that He rejoices when a sinner repents. The angels escort the righteous to await judgment. They will accompany Christ when He comes again and assist in gathering the saints, and separating the righteous from the wicked.

The Bible does not give us a great amount of specific, descriptive information regarding the angels. It is clear, however, that the appearance of an angel often caused people to be afraid. Perhaps the ancient belief that this meant certain death was responsible for such a reaction. Or it could be that the angel suddenly materialized before their eyes causing fear. It is also possible that the angels' countenance was so alarming that the natural response of human beings was panic.

When angels came to earth, they often took on human bodies in order to be seen by those to whom they were sent. The scarcity of descriptive information indicates to us that this knowledge lacks importance in our investigation.

Except for the superior position given to the archangel Michael, the angels of heaven are not graded or ranked in any way in the Scripture. In the Bible, only two angels, Michael and Gabriel, have proper names. Cherubim, seraphim, and living creatures are heavenly beings which exist in addition to, and separate from, the angels.

Angels were a part of every phase of the earthly life of Jesus Christ. They are with Him in heaven today and will join Him when He comes again. Christ was inferior to the angels at the time He became a mortal but His superiority was established again when He arose from death.

If there is any function which angels are performing to benefit man on earth today, it is not specified in the Scriptures. The record of appearances of angels to people on earth ended with the incidents set down in the Book of Acts.

When we seek the source of our misinformation concerning the angels, we must go back to the Babylonian captivity of the Jews. At that time they were exposed to pagan beliefs about the spirit world and began to exaggerate the role of angels. Later, the Persians also had a part in the corruption of the simple biblical truth about the angels. When the Jews accepted Greek culture, they continued to alter their beliefs regarding heaven's angels.

The uninspired, yet respected, writings of the Apocrypha and the Pseudepigrapha contributed to the amplification of the function of angels. Jewish authorative literature did nothing to correct the condition of confusion surrounding the angels.

The great works of classical art and literature compounded the problem of inaccuracy with reference to angels. As was noted earlier, the Bible did not describe angels in great detail. The artists turned to mythology for these particulars, and then illustrated mythological and biblical characters with so much similarity they were indistinguishable.

Because Dante and Milton wrote about biblical subjects, their writings received a semireligious position which is undeserved. Many well-educated people know (or think they know) more about the angels from *The Divine Comedy* and *Paradise Lost* than they do from the Bible.

When artists and authors were faced with the need to portray spiritual beings to mortal minds, they resorted to attributes which were contrived to portray the angels. These inventive minds imagined angels as physically attractive — even beautiful. They also equipped these spirit messengers with the wings of huge birds, and organized them into choirs which sang beautiful praises to God. Their creativity would not be complete without the halo, or circle of light about the head.

The religious beliefs of people in faraway lands as well as people in the next block may have contributed to our confused view of the angels. The Church of Jesus Christ of Latter-day Saints and Jehovah's Witnesses are among those not conforming to the teachings of Scripture with regard to doctrine on angels.

The Old Testament record did not reveal abundant information about the activities of Jesus Christ in ancient times. There was much evidence that He acted for God and appeared as an angel — the angel of the Lord. This angel was God Himself, but was separate from God the Father. The angel of the Lord was a function of God's Son before He became the man Jesus.

There was a character, born of superstition, called the "Death Angel." Although God sometimes sent His angels to take human life, there is no biblical record of a death angel. The Exodus account of the Ten Plagues did not mention a death angel or any other angel.

The guardian angel which many people believe is giving them spiritual direction and personal safety is not found in the pages of the books of Scripture. It was rather the product of the polytheistic belief of the Persians, Roman mythology, and Jewish tradition. Early Christians accepted the belief in guardian angels. From its beginning the Islamic religion taught a similar doctrine. The Roman Catholic Church along with the theologians and philosophers it produced, also embraced the guardian angel belief. Both apocryphal and pseudepigraphal books added to the erroneous information concerning this popular angel.

The Scripture mentions two kinds of evil angels; the angels who sinned and the angels of Satan. The Bible does not teach that the devil was once an angel, Lucifer, who sinned and was thrown out of heaven, becoming Satan. Nor does it inform us that the angels who sinned became the angels of Satan.

Much sentimentality is attached to the angelic images we hold. Often they are based on feelings rather than facts. We are satisfied with the picture we have in our minds. Most of us have attached a degree of security to our own personal concept of angels. We are comfortable in the knowledge that we cannot be wrong about such a familiar subject.

We also remind ourselves that this is not a subject which is necessary for our soul's salvation. So how much study and concern can it possibly deserve?

Despite the reality that we have a distorted version of heaven's angels in our minds we may still seek to justify our own opinion. To support our long-standing convictions, we take our own favorite persuasions and theories, which are not stated in the Bible, and look for some text or texts to defend them. When we find a verse which seems to apply, we are satisfied.

What is the source of your perception of God's angels? If you find that it cannot be supported by Scripture, where did it originate? Is it reliable? Should you continue to attempt to sustain it?

If you find that your information concerning the subject of God's holy angels is less than accurate, please examine the Scriptures more carefully as you investigate this and other topics in the future. Keep in mind, memory stores secular facts in the same file with scriptural knowledge, on a particular subject. You are responsible for separating them.

Bibliography

Adler, Mortimer J. *The Angels and Us.* New York: Macmillan, 1982.

Allegro, John. *The Mystery of the Dead Sea Scrolls Revealed.* New York: Gramercy, 1981.

Aquinas, Thomas. *The Summa Theologica.* Trans. Fathers of the English Dominican Province.

Bethany Parallel Commentary on the New Testament. Minneapolis, Minnesota: Bethany, 1983.

Bethany Parallel Commentary on the Old Testament. Minneapolis, Minnesota: Bethany, 1985.

Boles, H. Leo. *A Commentary on the Gospel According to Luke.* Nashville, Tennessee: Gospel Advocate, 1972.

Brandon, S.G.F. *Religion in Ancient History.* New York: Scribner's, 1969.

Bright, John. *A History of Israel.* Philadelphia: Westminster, 1959.

Brown, Stephanie. *Religious Painting.* New York: Mayflower, 1979.

Bruce, F.F. *The Books and the Parchments.* Old Tappan, New Jersey: Revel, 1963.

Bulfinch, Thomas. *Bulfinch's Mythology.* New York: Crowell, 1959.

Daiches, David. *A Critical History of English Literature.* New York: Ronald Press, 1960.

Dante Aligheri. *The Divine Comedy.*

Dickinson, Edward. *Music in the History of the Church.* 1969.

Dictionary of New Testament Theology. Grand Rapids, Michigan: Zondervan, 1975.

The Doctrine and Covenants. Salt Lake City, Utah: Church of Jesus Christ of Latter-day Saints, 1985.

Encyclopaedia Britannica. 1988.

The Encyclopaedia Judaica. Jerusalem, Israel: Macmillan, 1972.

The Forgotten Books of Eden. New York: Bell, 1981.

Ginzburg, Louis. Trans. Henrietta Szold. *The Legend of the Jews.* Philadelphia: Jewish Publications, 1909.

Green, Roger Lancelyn. *The Tale of Ancient Israel.* London: J.M. Dent, 1969.

Hamilton, Edith. *Mythology.* Boston, Massachusetts: Little, Brown, 1942.

Hobley, Leonard F. *Moslems and Islam.* East Sussex, England: Wayland, 1979.

Janson, H.W. *History of Art.* Englewood Cliffs, New Jersey: Prentice-Hall, 1985.

Josephus. *Antiquities.* Trans. William Whiston. Grand Rapids, Michigan: Kregel, 1978.

The Koran. Trans. N.J. Dawood. Middlesex, England: Penguin, 1974.

McConkie, Bruce R. *Mormon Doctrine.* Salt Lake City, Utah: Bookcraft, 1979.

Magnani, Duane. *The Watchtower Files.* Minneapolis, Minnesota: Bethany House, 1985.

McGuiggan, Jim. *The Book of Daniel.* Lubbock, Texas: Montex, 1978.

— — — *The Book of Ezekiel.* Lubbock, Texas: Montex, 1979.

— — — *The Book of Revelation.* Lubbock, Texas: Montex, 1978.

Milligan, Robert. *A Commentary on the Epistle to the Hebrews.* Nashville, Tennessee: Gospel Advocate, 1971.

Milton, John. *Paradise Lost.*

The Book of Mormon. Salt Lake City, Utah: Church of Jesus Christ of Latter-Day Saints, 1986.

New Analytical Bible. Chicago: Dickson, 1964.

The New American Bible for Catholics. Nashville, Tennessee: Nelson, 1983.

The NIV Study Bible. Grand Rapids, Michigan: Zondervan, 1985.

New Testament Apocrypha. Trans. R. McL. Wilson, Philadelphia: Westminster, 1963.

The NIV Study Bible. Grand Rapids, Michigan: Zondervan, 1985.

The Pearl of Great Price. Salt Lake City, Utah: Church of Jesus Christ of Latter-Day Saints, 1985.

Pfeiffer, Charles F. *Old Testament History.* Grand Rapids, Michigan: Baker, 1973.

Potter, Charles Francis. *The Great Religious Leaders.* New York: Simon and Schuster, 1958.

Rappoport, Angelo S., Ph.D. *Ancient Israel: Myths and Legends.* New York: Bonanza, 1987.

Shakespeare, William. *Hamlet.*

Smith, Wilson. *Old Testament History.* Joplin, Missouri: College Press, 1970.

Strong, James. *Dictionary of the Hebrew Bible.* Nashville, Tennessee: Abingdon, 1980.

Theological Dictionary of the New Testament. Grand Rapids, Michigan: Eerdman's, 1964.

Vine, W.E. *An Expository Dictionary of New Testament Words.* Old Tappan, New Jersey: Revell, 1966.

Webster's New Collegiate Dictionary. Springfield, Massachusetts: Merriam, 1981.

Webber, F.R. *Church Symbolism.* Detroit: Gale Research, 1971.

Woods, Guy N. *A Commentary on the New Testament Epistles of Peter, John, and Jude.* Nashville, Tennessee: Gospel Advocate, 1970.

You Can Live Forever in Paradise on Earth. Brooklyn, New York: Watchtower Bible and Tract Society, 1982.